Survey of Academic Library Practices
in Staging Special Events

ISBN: 978-1-57440-220-9
Library of Congress Control Number: 2013930448
© 2013 Primary Research Group, Inc.

TABLE OF CONTENTS

LIST OF TABLES

THE QUESTIONNAIRE

EVENT STATISTICS

1. How many of each of the following kinds of special events did the library present in the past year?

    A. Readings
    B. Musical performances
    C. Theatrical performances
    D. Lectures or speeches
    E. Film or movie showings
    F. Fairs
    G. Exhibits
    H. Auctions

2. If your library hosted any other kinds of special events in the past year, what were they and how many did they host?

3. Does the library have a budget specifically for events?

4. If so, what is this budget?

5. Which departments of the library stage the most events and approximately how many do they stage each year?

6. How many events did the library present in each of the following years?

    A. 2011
    B. 2012
    C. 2013 (anticipated)

REVENUE AND ATTENDANCE

7. For what percentage of events does the library charge admission?

8. What was the total attendance at all library-sponsored events in the past year?

9. What is the average attendance for each of the following types of events?

    A. Readings
    B. Musical performances

    C.   Theatrical performances
    D.   Lectures or speeches
    E.   Film or movie showings
    F.   Fairs
    G.   Exhibits
    H.   Auctions
    I.   All other

10. What were the total revenues from the following sources through library events in the past year?

    A.   Admission fees for tickets
    B.   Donations specifically to attend fundraising events

MOST EFFECTIVE EVENTS

11. What are some of the library's most effective events in terms of raising the awareness level of library patrons or in raising money through donations or admission fees?

12. If your library shows films, what was the most popular film or film series presented by the library over the past three years?

13. If your library holds book readings, what was the most popular reading that your library has staged over the past three years?

STAFFING & FOOD SERVICE

14. How does the library staff special events? Does the library incur additional fees for security, food service, usher services, or other personnel costs? What are the costs and how are they paid for?

15. Does the library have an events coordinator or director who manages many of the executive functions of event preparation, marketing, and deployment?

16. How does the library generally handle food service at library special events?

    A.   Does not offer food service
    B.   Provided by the college food service
    C.   Provided by the library café
    D.   Provided by outside caterers

17. What was the library's spending for food service at all special events in the past year?

DEPARTMENTAL HELP

18. Which academic or administrative departments of the college have partnered with the library to present special events at the library?

19. Which departments of the college or other parent organization are essential as partners in managing a library-sponsored event?

MARKETING LIBRARY SPECIAL EVENTS

20. Do various library departments share lists of attendees of library special events for marketing purposes?

21. Are attendees at library special events generally encouraged or required to provide contact information such as addresses and email addresses so that the library can use them for event marketing purposes?

22. How useful to your institution are the following marketing vehicles in advertising library special events?

     A.   Opt-in emails
     B.   Ads in college newspapers
     C.   Ads in commercial newspapers
     D.   Postings on blogs and listservs
     E.   Facebook or similar sites
     F.   Twitter or similar sites
     G.   YouTube or similar sites
     H.   Pinterest or similar sites
     I.   Library website
     J.   Posters and flyers
     K.   Presentations by librarians
     L.   Emails to faculty and staff of the institution

23. What is your most effective way of marketing library special events?

LIBRARY EVENTS STAGED OUTSIDE THE LIBRARY

24. How many special events sponsored at least in part by the library were held outside the library in the past year?

25. Please describe these events.

26. What was the approximate space rental costs, if any, for these events? If space was donated, mention this.

27. Approximately how many events that might be described as fundraisers did the library hold in the past year (including auctions, dinners, and any events designed to solicit donations or charity-related sales for the library)?

28. If the library did host any of these fundraising events, what percentage of the events were held in the library itself?

RECORDS AND ARCHIVES OF LIBRARY SPECIAL EVENTS

29. Are any library special events photographed or videotaped? If so, how do you use these photos or tapes and where are they presented or archived?

30. If photos, video or audio tapes, or text transcripts of library special events are archived or otherwise maintained, has the library developed metadata or other finding aids so that these archives can be easily used? If so, how have you done this?

SURVEY PARTICIPANTS

Alma College
Baton Rouge Community College
Bryan College
Calvin College – Hekman Library
Christendom College Library
Coastal Carolina University
Colorado State University
Eastern Kentucky University Libraries
Ferris State University
Institute of American Indian Arts
Jackson State Community College
Mott Community College
Mount Saint Mary College
Northwestern University Library
Riemenschneider Bach Institute
Savannah College Art Design, Atlanta Campus
SUNY Canton – Southworth Library
SUNY Fredonia – Daniel A. Reed Library
The University of Texas at San Antonio
UCLA College Library
UMass Libraries
University of Arizona Libraries, Special Collections
University of Guam
University of Michigan
University of Mississippi
University of Nebraska-Lincoln
University of New Hampshire Library
University of North Texas
University of Southern Indiana Rice Library
University of Texas Libraries

CHARACTERISTICS OF THE SAMPLE

Overall sample size: 31

By Public or Private Status

Public	23
Private	8

By Type of College

Community college	4
4-year college	11
MA- or PhD-granting college	7
Research university	9

By Average Annual Full-Time Student Tuition

Less than $10,000	12
$10,000 to $19,999	10
$20,000 or more	9

By Full-Time Equivalent Enrollment

Less than 5,000	11
5,000 to 19,999	11
20,000 or more	9

**By Total Number of Special Events Presented
 by the Library in the Past Year**

Less than 10	15
10 or more	16

Public or private status of the college, broken out by type of college.

Type of College	Public	Private
Community college	100.00%	0.00%
4-year college	45.45%	54.55%
MA-/PhD-granting college	100.00%	0.00%
Research university	77.78%	22.22%

Public or private status of the college, broken out by average annual full-time student tuition.

Tuition	Public	Private
Less than $10,000	91.67%	8.33%
$10,000 to $19,999	90.00%	10.00%
$20,000 or more	33.33%	66.67%

Public or private status of the college, broken out by full-time equivalent enrollment.

Enrollment	Public	Private
Less than 5,000	45.45%	54.55%
5,000 to 19,999	90.91%	9.09%
20,000 or more	88.89%	11.11%

Public or private status of the college, broken out by total number of special events presented by the library in the past year.

Number of Events	Public	Private
Less than 10	60.00%	40.00%
10 or more	87.50%	12.50%

Type of college, broken out by public or private status of the college.

Public or Private	Community college	4-year college	MA-/PhD-granting college	Research university
Public	17.39%	21.74%	30.43%	30.43%
Private	0.00%	75.00%	0.00%	25.00%

Type of college, broken out by average annual full-time student tuition.

Tuition	Community college	4-year college	MA-/PhD-granting college	Research university
Less than $10,000	33.33%	25.00%	25.00%	16.67%
$10,000 to $19,999	0.00%	20.00%	30.00%	50.00%
$20,000 or more	0.00%	66.67%	11.11%	22.22%

Type of college, broken out by full-time equivalent enrollment.

Enrollment	Community college	4-year college	MA-/PhD-granting college	Research university
Less than 5,000	18.18%	72.73%	9.09%	0.00%
5,000 to 19,999	18.18%	27.27%	36.36%	18.18%
20,000 or more	0.00%	0.00%	22.22%	77.78%

Type of college, broken out by total number of special events presented by the library in the past year.

Number of Events	Community college	4-year college	MA-/PhD-granting college	Research university
Less than 10	13.33%	46.67%	26.67%	13.33%
10 or more	12.50%	25.00%	18.75%	43.75%

Average annual full-time student tuition, broken out by public or private status of the college.

Public or Private	Less than $10,000	$10,000 to $19,999	$20,000 or more
Public	47.83%	39.13%	13.04%
Private	12.50%	12.50%	75.00%

Average annual full-time student tuition, broken out by type of college.

Type of College	Less than $10,000	$10,000 to $19,999	$20,000 or more
Community college	100.00%	0.00%	0.00%
4-year college	27.27%	18.18%	54.55%
MA-/PhD-granting college	42.86%	42.86%	14.29%
Research university	22.22%	55.56%	22.22%

Average annual full-time student tuition, broken out by full-time equivalent enrollment.

Enrollment	Less than $10,000	$10,000 to $19,999	$20,000 or more
Less than 5,000	27.27%	18.18%	54.55%
5,000 to 19,999	54.55%	27.27%	18.18%
20,000 or more	33.33%	55.56%	11.11%

Average annual full-time student tuition, broken out by total number of special events presented by the library in the past year.

Number of Events	Less than $10,000	$10,000 to $19,999	$20,000 or more
Less than 10	33.33%	26.67%	40.00%
10 or more	43.75%	37.50%	18.75%

Full-time equivalent enrollment, broken out by public or private status of the college.

Public or Private	Less than 5,000	5,000 to 19,999	20,000 or more
Public	21.74%	43.48%	34.78%
Private	75.00%	12.50%	12.50%

Full-time equivalent enrollment, broken out by type of college.

Type of College	Less than 5,000	5,000 to 19,999	20,000 or more
Community college	50.00%	50.00%	0.00%
4-year college	72.73%	27.27%	0.00%
MA-/PhD-granting college	14.29%	57.14%	28.57%
Research university	0.00%	22.22%	77.78%

Full-time equivalent enrollment, broken out by average annual full-time student tuition.

Tuition	Less than 5,000	5,000 to 19,999	20,000 or more
Less than $10,000	25.00%	50.00%	25.00%
$10,000 to $19,999	20.00%	30.00%	50.00%
$20,000 or more	66.67%	22.22%	11.11%

Full-time equivalent enrollment, broken out by total number of special events presented by the library in the past year.

Number of Events	Less than 5,000	5,000 to 19,999	20,000 or more
Less than 10	60.00%	33.33%	6.67%
10 or more	12.50%	37.50%	50.00%

Total number of special events presented by the library in the past year, broken out by public or private status of the college.

Public or Private	Less than 10	10 or more
Public	39.13%	60.87%
Private	75.00%	25.00%

Total number of special events presented by the library in the past year, broken out by type of college.

Type of College	Less than 10	10 or more
Community college	50.00%	50.00%
4-year college	63.64%	36.36%
MA-/PhD-granting college	57.14%	42.86%
Research university	22.22%	77.78%

Total number of special events presented by the library in the past year, broken out by average annual full-time student tuition.

Tuition	Less than 10	10 or more
Less than $10,000	41.67%	58.33%
$10,000 to $19,999	40.00%	60.00%
$20,000 or more	66.67%	33.33%

Total number of special events presented by the library in the past year, broken out by full-time equivalent enrollment.

Enrollment	Less than 10	10 or more
Less than 5,000	81.82%	18.18%
5,000 to 19,999	45.45%	54.55%
20,000 or more	11.11%	88.89%

If you are giving data and responses for particular departments, what are they?*

1. College (undergraduate) library.

2. Bach Institute Library.

3. Special Collections.

4. Shelving.

5. Special Collections.

6. Public Services Division.

7. Undergraduate library. Graduate library.

8. Marketing.

9. Archives & Special Collections.

---

* If you have consolidated library-wide data we prefer it, but if you give data for specific departments or a single department then all questions that ask for "library" data may be construed for your purposes to be data for the departments that you specify and not for your entire library.

SUMMARY OF MAIN FINDINGS

EVENT STATISTICS

We asked survey participants how many of each of the following kinds of events were presented by the library in the past year: readings; musical performances; theatrical performances; lectures or speeches; film or movie showings; fairs; exhibits; and auctions.

Readings

The libraries in the sample hosted a mean of 2.43 readings each in the past year. The median here was 1, and the range was from 0 to 10. Public schools had a higher mean (2.59) than private schools (2), although the median was larger for the latter group than it was for the former (1.5 to 1). Broken out by type of college, the means are fairly consistent, from a low of 2.25 for community colleges to a high of 2.57 for MA-/PhD-granting colleges, although 4-year colleges posted a median of 3, the highest of the group and twice that of the next closest median. Whereas schools with an average annual tuition under $10,000 hosted a mean of 1.36 readings, those schools where the tuition was $10,000 to $19,999 hosted a mean of 3.3. As could be expected, the frequency of these readings increases as school size increases, from a mean of 2 for those schools with less than 5,000 students to a mean of 3.11 for those with 20,000 or more students.

Musical and Theatrical Performances

The libraries in the sample hosted a mean of 1.23 musical performances in the past year. The median, however, was 0. While public schools hosted a mean of 1.5 and a max of 16 such events, private schools had a mean of 0.5 and a max of just 2. Broken out by type of college, the research universities well outpaced the rest of the pack, with a mean of 2.89 and a median of 2. All other medians in this category were 0, and the next closest mean belonged to 4-year colleges at 0.8. As total enrollment increased, so too did the number of musical performances presented by the library, up to a mean of 2.78 for those with 20,000 or more students. The mean for those schools with less than 5,000 students was a paltry 0.18.

Only five libraries in the sample presented any theatrical performances over the past year, and none hosted more than four.

Lectures or Speeches

The libraries in the sample presented a mean of 5.9 lectures/speeches in the past year, with one library hosting as many as 40 such events. The overall median was 2. Public schools had a mean nearly twice that of private schools, 6.77 to 3.5, as well as a median of 4 compared to the latter's median of 1.5. The research universities presented the most of these kinds of events: with a mean of 12.22 and a median of 12, both figures were higher than the maximum for any other type of college. The next closest were the MA-/PhD-granting colleges, with a mean of 4.43 and a median of 4. The schools where the average annual tuition was greater than $20,000 presented a mean of 8.22 lectures and speeches, while those schools where tuition was below $10,000 had a mean of 4.73. Likewise, the largest schools (those with 20,000 or more students) had the highest mean at 12, while the smallest schools (less than 5,000 students) hosted a mean of just 1.91 such events over the past year.

Film and Movie Showings

Only eight libraries in the sample hosted film or movie showings in the past year, with just three of those having more than three each (the maximum was 20). The overall sample mean was 1.53. All of these participants were public schools that hosted 10 or more special events each year. Those schools with the lowest average tuition were the most active in this respect, as those with tuitions less than $10,000 had a mean of 2.09 and those in the $10,000 to $19,999 range had a mean of 2. On the other side of the spectrum were the schools with an average tuition of $20,000 or greater, which hosted a mean of just 0.33 film and movie showings in the past year. No libraries in the sample at 4-year colleges hosted any of these events, while community colleges hosted a mean of just 0.5.

Exhibits

Exhibits proved to be the most popular type of event presented by the libraries in the sample, with an overall sample mean of 6.27 and a median of 3.5 (both the highest among all types of events). In fact, all but three survey participants hosted at least one such event over the past year, with one library hosting as many as 50 exhibits. The public schools compiled a mean more than twice that of their private school counterparts, 7.36 to 3.25. Broken out by type of college, the libraries at community colleges were the most active here, presenting a mean of 10.5 exhibits in the past year. The median was 10. The next closest mean and median was 6.8 and 5, respectively. Those schools with the lowest average tuition (less than $10,000) hosted a mean of 9.82 exhibits, more than double the next closest mean of 4.56.

Fairs and Auctions

Only 11 libraries in the sample presented any fairs in the past year, and just one of those libraries hosted more than two such fairs (it hosted six). Just one library in the sample presented any auctions, of which it presented just one.

Library Events Budget

25.81 percent of libraries in the sample have a budget specifically for events. The split between public and private schools is nearly identical (26.09 percent for the former, 25 percent for the latter), as is the split between those libraries that host less than 10 events per year (26.67 percent) and those libraries that host 10 or more events (25 percent). A noticeable gap appears when the data is broken out by type of college: whereas 44.44 percent of research university libraries have a specific events budget, this is true for just 18.18 percent of 4-year colleges and 14.29 percent of MA-/PhD-granting colleges in the sample. A third of all the libraries at schools with an enrollment of 20,000 or greater have an events budget, compared to just 18.18 percent of those schools in the 5,000 to 19,999 enrollment range.

For Those libraries that do have an events budget, the mean budget is $7,200. The median here is $10,000, while the range is from a minimum of $600 to a max of $15,000. Public schools have, on average, larger budgets than private schools, with means of $7,920 and $5,400, respectively. Broken out by type of college, the research universities are the big spenders here, with a mean budget of $11,750. By comparison, the next closest mean belongs to the 4-year colleges at $1,400. In fact, the minimum for research universities is $10,000, while no other school has a budget higher than $2,000.

Events by Year

The libraries in the sample presented a mean of 14.97 events in 2011, a figure that rose to 18.5 in 2012 and is expected to rise again to 20.27 in 2013. For all three years, the means for public schools outdistanced those of private schools: 17.74 to 5.86 in 2011, 21.52 to 8.57 in 2012, and 23.98 to 9.14 in 2013. Broken out by type of college, the community colleges in the sample expect to see the most growth here as their mean of 7.75 in 2011 will nearly double by 2013 (to 13.13). However, the community colleges still hold, on average, the fewest number of events, while research universities hold the most, a mean of 30.13 in 2012. 4-year colleges and MA-/PhD-granting colleges are half that total at 14.91 and 14.86, respectively. In 2011, there wasn't much of a difference in the number of events held when the data is broken out by average tuition, with the lowest mean coming from the "less than $10,000" range (14.5) and the highest coming from the $20,000 or more" range (15.38). This gap widens a bit in 2012, with a high mean of 20.9 and a low of 16.63. As could be expected, the number of events presented by the libraries in the sample steadily increases as total enrollment increases. In 2011, those libraries at schools with less than 5,000 students presented a mean of 5.64 events, while those in the "5,000 to 19,999" enrollment range had a mean of 15.3 and those in the "20,000 or more" range a mean of 26. All these figures increase from year to year, although none as drastically as the numbers for the schools with less than 5,000 students: by 2013, they expect to nearly double the number of events they present, a mean of 10.27.

REVENUE AND ATTENDANCE

Admission Fees

Just six libraries in the sample charge admission fees for any of their sponsored events. Of these six (all of which are public schools with at least 5,000 students), none of them charge for more than 5 percent of their total events. Overall, this means the libraries in the sample charge admission for a mean of 0.63 percent of all library events.

Total Attendance

We asked survey participants what was the total attendance at all library-sponsored events in the past year. The overall mean was 1,198, although the median was nearly half that at 600. The range was from a low of 80 attendees to a maximum of 5,000. The events at the libraries of the public schools in the sample were significantly more popular than those at private schools, with a mean of 1,501 for the former and a mean of 421 for the latter. On average, community colleges (mean of 483) and 4-year colleges (601) attracted fewer people than MA-/PhD-granting colleges (1,783) and research universities (1,967). Broken out by average tuition, those schools in the middle range ($10,000 to $19,999) averaged much higher attendance levels than all others, with a mean of 1,766, while those schools in the bottom and top ranges had means of 938 and 921, respectively. As enrollment increases, so too does the attendance at these library-sponsored events, from a mean of 421 for those schools with less than 5,000 students up to a mean of 2,225 for the "20,000 or more" enrollment range.

Attendance at Readings

The libraries in the sample attract a mean of 54 people for each library-sponsored reading. The median is 30, and while one participant says such events are attended by just one person, the maximum is 300. These events are more popular with public schools, which attract a mean of 62 people, as compared to private schools where the mean is just 29. Broken out by type of college, the biggest turnouts are at the MA-/PhD-granting colleges, where the mean is 135 and the median is 100. The next closest are the 4-year colleges (a mean of 42 and median of 43). The libraries at the biggest schools (those with 20,000 or more students) draw a mean of 105 people to these events, while those at the smallest schools (less than 5,000 students) have a mean of just 34.

Attendance at Musical Performances

The libraries in the sample attract a mean of 40 people to each musical performance. The median is 30 and the maximum is 100. Public schools again attract more than private schools, with a mean of 44 for the former and a mean of 10 for the latter, while research universities have the highest average attendance among all types of colleges with a mean of 53. By comparison, the next closest mean belongs to the 4-year colleges at 36. Those libraries at schools where the tuition is between $10,000 and $20,000 have a mean attendance of 70 for these events, while those where tuition is $20,000 or more attract a mean of just 15. Whereas the mean attendance at musical performances for those schools with a total enrollment less than 5,000 is 10, this figure jumps up to 44 for the next enrollment range (5,000 to 19,999) where it plateaus at 43.75 for the top enrollment range (20,000 or more students).

Attendance at Theatrical Performances

The attendance numbers for theatrical performances are similar to those for musical performances, with an overall sample mean of 37 and a median of 40. Public schools attract roughly the same amount of people for these events as they did for musical performances (a mean of 47), although the mean attendance for private schools jumps to 22.5. As with musical performances, no community colleges in the sample offer any theatrical performances, nor do any MA-/PhD-granting colleges. When broken out by total student enrollment, attendance increases steadily as enrollment increases: for those schools with less than 5,000 students, the mean is 20; for those with 5,000 to 19,999 students, the mean jumps to 32.5; and for those with 20,000 or more students, the mean is 50. No library in the sample that hosted less than 10 events held a theatrical performance.

Attendance at Lectures or Speeches

The libraries in the sample attracted a mean of 57 people to lectures and speeches. The median was 40, and the range was from a minimum of 10 to a maximum of 300. These events were most popular with libraries at private schools, as they attracted a mean of 105 people compared to a mean of 45 people for public schools. The medians, however, were much closer: 50 for the former, and 40 for the latter. Broken out by type of college, the research universities in the sample attracted the most people, a mean of 97.5. The next closest mean belonged to MA-/PhD-granting colleges at 52. As average annual tuition increase, the average attendance at lectures and speeches decreased, from a mean of 66 for those in the "less than $10,000" range, all the way down to a mean of 38 for those in the "$20,000 or more" range. Libraries at schools with 20,000 or more students attracted a mean of 83 people to these events while those at schools with less than 5,000 students attracted a mean of 37.5. Those libraries that hosted the least number of events (less than 10) had the highest attendance levels, a mean of 81, while those libraries that hosted 10 or more events had a mean of just 42.

Attendance at Film or Movie Showings

The libraries in the sample attracted a mean of 36 people to film or movie showings. The median was 21.5, and the range was from a minimum of five to a maximum of 150. No libraries at private schools in the sample hosted these film or movie showings. Research universities once again outdistanced the pack with a mean of 45. As enrollment increases, so too does attendance at these events, from a mean of 15 for those libraries at schools with less than 5,000 students to a mean of 42 for those libraries and schools with 20,000 or more students. No libraries that held less than 10 events hosted any movie or film showings.

Attendance at Fairs

The libraries in the sample attracted a mean of 88 people to fairs. These were more popular with private school libraries, which attracted a mean of 127.5 people, than they were with public school libraries, which attracted a mean of 80 people. The medians also favored the private schools, 127.5 to 44. Yet again, the research universities attract the most guests, a mean of 171. By comparison, the next closest mean belongs to the 4-year colleges with a mean of 63. For libraries at schools where the average tuition is less than $10,000, the mean is 50. This more than doubles for the next tuition range ($10,000 to $19,999) to 104 and increases further still for the top tuition range ($20,000 or more) to a mean of 115. Broken out by total enrollment, the largest schools (those with 20,000 or more students) attract a mean of 171 people to fairs, while those in the middle range (5,000 to 19,999 students) post a mean of just 40.

Attendance at Auctions

Only one survey participant hosted any auctions, which attract a mean of 75 people.

Total Revenue from Admission Fees and Donations

Only one library in the sample collected any revenues from admission fees to library events in the past year. This participant collected $500. Only three libraries collected any revenues from donations to attend fund-raising events. These three libraries collected a mean of $1,100.

STAFFING & FOOD SERVICE

Nearly half (48.39 percent) of the libraries in the sample do not have an events coordinator or director who manages many of the executive functions of event preparation, marketing, and deployment. The majority of libraries that do have such coordinators are those libraries at private schools, where 62.5 percent of them do. While no community colleges in the sample have such a coordinator, 77.78 percent of research universities do. So too do 77.78 percent of libraries at schools with 20,000 or more students, while just 27.27 percent of those libraries at schools with less than 5,000 students do. Libraries that host 10 or more events each year are more likely to have these coordinators, as 56.25 percent of them to compared to just a third of those libraries that presented less than 10 events last year.

Food Service at Special Events

We asked survey participants how the library handles food service at special events. The majority (51.61 percent) say this is handled by the college food service. No participants say food service at these events is handled by the library café, while 22.58 percent say it is provided by outside caterers and an identical 22.58 percent say they do not offer food service. Private schools are more likely not to offer food service, as 50 percent do not. Broken out by type of college, 4-year colleges are the least likely to use outside caterers as just 9.09 percent of them do. On the other end of the spectrum, outside caterers are used by 25 percent of community colleges, 28.57 percent of MA-/PhD-granting colleges, and 33.33 percent of research universities. As average tuition rises, the library becomes less likely to use the college food service: 66.67 percent of libraries at schools where the average tuition is less than $10,000 use the college food service at these special events, a figure which drops down to 50 percent for the next tuition range ($10,000 to $19,999) and then down further to 33.33 percent for the top tuition range ($20,000 or more). 44.44 percent of libraries at schools with the enrollment is at least 20,000 use outside caterers for these events, compared to just 9.09 percent of those libraries at schools with enrollments under 5,000.

Libraries in the sample spent a mean of $1,992 last year on food service for special events. The median was $350, and while five participants did not spend at all in this respect, seven participants spent at least $1,000, with one library spending as much as $16,500. Libraries at public schools spent considerably more than those at private schools, with a mean of $2,442 for the former and a mean of $642 for the latter. Broken out by type of college, community colleges and 4-year colleges both had means of around $200, while research universities spent a mean of $4,339 on food services at events last year. The largest schools (those with 20,000 or more students) spent a mean of $4,861 in this respect, while no other range in this category had a mean higher than $375. For those libraries that had 10 or more events in the past year, mean spending on food services was $3,032, while those libraries with less than 10 events spent a mean of $535.

MARKETING LIBRARY SPECIAL EVENTS

Attendance and Marketing Efforts

70.97 percent of libraries in the sample do not share lists of attendees of library special events for marketing purposes, while 22.58 percent of them do. The majority of these libraries that do share lists are at research universities, as 66.67 percent of them practice this. On the other hand, no community colleges or MA-/PhD-granting colleges share these lists, and only 9.09 percent of 4-year colleges do. Two-thirds of survey participants at schools with 20,000 or more students share attendance lists for marketing purposes, while just 9.09 percent of those with enrollments less than 5,000 do this. No libraries at schools in the "5,000 to 19,999" enrollment range share these lists. Whereas 31.25 percent of those libraries that hosted 10 or more events last year share these lists with library departments, just 13.33 percent of those libraries that hosted less than 10 events can say the same.

Marketing Vehicles

We asked survey participants how useful the following Marketing vehicles are in advertising library special events: opt-in emails; ads in college newspapers; ads in commercial newspapers; postings on blogs and listservs; Facebook or similar sites; Twitter or similar sites; YouTube or similar sites; Pinterest or similar sites; library website; posters and flyers; presentations by librarians; and emails to faculty and staff of the institution.

The Library Website, Posters and Flyers, and Emails to Faculty and Staff

The library website, posters and flyers, and emails to faculty and staff proved to be the most useful marketing vehicles available to the libraries in the sample. At least 80 percent of all survey participants considered these three marketing vehicles to be either "useful" or "critical." All of the private schools in the sample considered posters and flyers to be "useful" or "critical," as did all the research universities and those schools where the average tuition is $20,000 or more. No libraries in the sample thought this to be "rarely useful" or "not useful." 52.17 percent of public schools in the sample found the library website to be "critical" in terms of marketing while just 37.5 percent of private schools thought this to be the case. This was also popular for 4-year colleges, as 54.55 percent thought this to be "critical," as did 58.33 percent of those schools where the average tuition is less than $10,000. More than half of all survey participants found emails to faculty and staff of the institution to be "critical" for marketing reasons. Such emails are especially popular with public schools as 65.22 percent of them think these emails are "critical" for marketing purposes as compared to just 12.5 percent of private schools. So too do 75 percent of those libraries at schools where the average tuition is less than $10,000.

Blogs, Facebook, and Presentations by Librarians

Postings on blogs and listservs, the use of Facebook (and similar social networking sites), and presentations by librarians are also well regarded in terms of their marketing values as between 40 and 55 percent of all survey participants think these three vehicles to be either "useful" or "critical." Of the three, Facebook proves to be the most popular, a little bit more than postings on blogs and listservs, although for both categories 22.58 percent of the sample find these to be "critical" to marketing the library's special events. However, 32.26 percent find Facebook to be "useful," as compared to 25.81 percent for postings on blogs and listservs. 18.18 percent of 4-year colleges either find Facebook to be "not useful" or do not use it at all, as do 14.29 percent of MA-/PhD-granting colleges. While 63.64 percent of those schools with less than 5,000 students find Facebook to be "useful" in this respect, none in this category thought it "critical" and 27.27 percent thought it to be "not useful." All of the libraries in the sample at schools with 20,000 or more students found Facebook to be at least "somewhat useful," as did all those libraries that hosted 10 or more events in the past year. On the other hand, those libraries that hosted less than 10 events in the past year found Facebook to be "rarely useful" 13.33 percent of the time, while 20 percent of these participants thought it to be "not useful." Concerning presentations by librarians, this tactic was found "useful" by 71.43 percent of MA-/PhD-granting libraries in the sample. Broken out by public or private status, the private schools relied on these presentations much less than public schools: just 12.5 percent of the former rated them as "useful" and none thought them to be "critical," while 52.17 percent of the latter thought these presentations to be at least "useful." Nearly half (44.44 percent) of those libraries in the sample at schools where the average tuition is $20,000 or more find presentations by librarians to be either "rarely useful" or "not useful," and none find it to be "critical." These presentations are favored more by those schools with an average tuition of less than $10,000, as 50 percent find them to be at least "useful."

Opt-in Emails

Opt-in emails were found to be "not useful" by 45.16 percent of the sample, although 12.9 percent did think of them as "critical" and another 19.35 percent found them to be "useful." None of those participants that thought these emails to be "critical" were from private schools, although 37.5 percent of private schools did find them to be "useful." While 17.39 percent of public schools rated opt-in emails as "critical," nearly half (47.83 percent) deemed them "not useful." 71.43 percent of MA-/PhD-granting colleges either didn't use opt-in emails or found them to be "not useful." Another 14.29 percent thought them to be "rarely useful." These were more popular at schools with higher enrollments, as 55.55 percent of those libraries at schools with 20,000 or more students thought them to be either "useful" or "critical," compared to just 18.18 percent of those schools with less than 5,000 students. Similarly, libraries that hosted less than 10 events last year found these "useful" or "critical" just 20 percent of the time, compared to 43.75 percent of those libraries that hosted 10 or more events.

Ads in Commercial Newspapers

The majority of survey participants (58.06 percent) found ads in commercial newspapers to be "not useful" in terms of marketing the library's special events. Just 6.45 percent thought them to be "critical" (all public schools with an average tuition under $20,000), and 9.68 percent thought them "useful." No schools with less than 5,000 students found these ads to be "useful" or "critical" to the library's marketing strategy, while 18.18 percent of those libraries at schools with an enrollment of 5,000 to 19,999 thought them "critical." An overwhelming 77.78 percent of schools where the tuition is $20,000 or more found these to be "not useful."

34

Twitter and Ads in College Newspapers

The use of Twitter (and other such sites) and ads in college newspapers are of similar usefulness to our survey participants: for both vehicles, 25-26 percent of all survey participants rated them as either "useful" or "critical," although no participant thought ads in college newspapers to be "critical" (compared to 6.45 percent for the use of Twitter). Whereas 50 percent of all participating private schools thought Twitter was "not useful," this was true of just 21.74 percent of public schools surveyed. The opposite is true for ads in college newspapers: 25 percent of private schools find these to be "not useful," while 47.83 percent of public schools rated them this way. Just 14.29 percent of all MA-/PhD-granting colleges in the sample find ads in college newspapers to be "useful," while the remaining 85.71 percent think these are either "rarely useful" or "not useful." However, 28.57 percent of these libraries find Twitter to be "critical" to library marketing, the only type of college to rate Twitter this way. More than half (54.55 percent) of the libraries in the sample at schools with less than 5,000 students find Twitter to be "not useful," while 45.45 percent of these same schools find ads in college newspapers to be "not useful" as well. Those libraries that hosted more than 10 events last year find Twitter to be a bit more useful than those libraries that hosted less than 10 events, as 37.5 percent of the former rated it as "somewhat useful" and another 25 percent rated it as "useful," compared to just 6.67 percent and 13.33 percent of the latter, respectively.

YouTube, Pinterest, and Other Such Sites

Sites such as YouTube and Pinterest proved to be the least useful to our survey participants, as no library in the sample rated either of these two sites (or sites like them) as "critical" or even "useful." In fact, 48.39 percent voted YouTube as "not useful," while 58.06 percent of the sample rated Pinterest the same way. 75 percent of private schools think YouTube to be "not useful," and 87.5 percent of these same schools view Pinterest in the same light. For schools with less than 5,000 students, 63.64 percent say YouTube is "not useful," and an identical 63.64 percent say the same about Pinterest. While 77.78 percent of those schools with 20,000 or more students say this about Pinterest, the remaining 22.22 percent did rate it as "somewhat useful," along with 27.27 percent of those schools in the "5,000 to 19,999" enrollment range. 50 percent of all libraries in the sample that hosted 10 or more events in the past year find YouTube to be "somewhat useful" in the library's marketing efforts.

LIBRARY EVENTS STAGED OUTSIDE THE LIBRARY

Number of Events Held Outside the Library

According to our survey participants, a mean of 2.31 events sponsored at least in part by the library were held outside the library in the past year. The median was 1, and the range was from 0 to 30. Public schools held, on average, 2.95 such events, while the mean for private schools was 0.63. In fact, no library at a private school held more than 2 events outside the library. Broken out by type of college, the research universities (mean of 2.44) and the 4-year colleges (3.3) were the most active in this respect, while MA-/PhD-granting colleges and community colleges hosted a mean of just 1.29 and 1, respectively. As average tuition increased, the number of these events decreased: from a mean of 3.9 for those schools with an average tuition less than \$10,000, to a mean of 2.3 for the middle range (\$10,000 to \$19,999) and finally a mean of 0.56 for the top range (\$20,000 or more). No library in the sample that had less than 10 events in the past year had more than 3 such events held outside the library (for a mean of 0.57), while those libraries that did host 10 or more events hosted a mean of 3.93 of them outside the library.

Fundraisers

Only 11 libraries in the sample (all public schools) held any fundraisers in the past year. This includes auctions, dinners, and any events designed to solicit donations or charity-related sales for the library. Of these 11, just one held more than four such events, while six of them hosted exactly one. The overall sample mean was 1.14, and the median was 0. The maximum was 15, belonging to a research university with 20,000 or more students. As total enrollment increases, so too does the number of these fundraisers, from a mean of 0.1 for the "less than 5,000" enrollment group, up to a mean of 0.89 for the next range (5,000 to 19,999 students) and finally all the way up to a mean of 2.56 for the top enrollment range (20,000 or more students). Just two libraries in the sample that had hosted less than 10 events in the past year had hosted any fundraisers during that time, both of which held just one such event. On the other hand, those libraries that hosted 10 or more events over the course of the last year held a mean of 2 fundraisers.

Among those 11 libraries in the sample that did host any sort of fundraiser over the last year, a mean of 46.54 percent of these events were held in the library itself. However, the range was broad, from a minimum of 1 percent to a max of 100. Four participants answered "100 percent," while another four answered "1 percent." Two participants said that 50 percent of these events were held at the library, while the remaining participant cited this at 7 percent. Among those 11 total participants, the highest mean when broken out by type of college was for the research universities, with a mean of 70.2 percent, while 4-year colleges had a mean of 53.5 percent. The split between those libraries that hosted less than 10 events in the past year and those that hosted 10 or more was fairly even: a mean of 50.5 percent for the former group, and 45.56 for the latter.

Chapter 1: Event Statistics

Table 1.1: How many of each of the following kinds of special events did the library present in the past year?

Table 1.1A: Readings

	Mean	Median	Minimum	Maximum
Entire sample	2.43	1.00	0.00	10.00

Table 1.1B: Musical performances

	Mean	Median	Minimum	Maximum
Entire sample	1.23	0.00	0.00	16.00

Table 1.1C: Theatrical performances

	Mean	Median	Minimum	Maximum
Entire sample	0.37	0.00	0.00	4.00

Table 1.1D: Lectures or speeches

	Mean	Median	Minimum	Maximum
Entire sample	5.90	2.00	0.00	40.00

Table 1.1E: Film or movie showings

	Mean	Median	Minimum	Maximum
Entire sample	1.53	0.00	0.00	20.00

Table 1.1F: Fairs

	Mean	Median	Minimum	Maximum
Entire sample	0.70	0.00	0.00	6.00

Table 1.1G: Exhibits

	Mean	Median	Minimum	Maximum
Entire sample	6.27	3.50	0.00	50.00

Table 1.1H: Auctions

	Mean	Median	Minimum	Maximum
Entire sample	0.03	0.00	0.00	1.00

Table 1.2: How many of each of the following kinds of special events did the library present in the past year? Broken out by public or private status of the college.

Table 1.2A: Readings

Public or Private	Mean	Median	Minimum	Maximum
Public	2.59	1.00	0.00	10.00
Private	2.00	1.50	0.00	5.00

Table 1.2B: Musical performances

Public or Private	Mean	Median	Minimum	Maximum
Public	1.50	0.00	0.00	16.00
Private	0.50	0.00	0.00	2.00

Table 1.2C: Theatrical performances

Public or Private	Mean	Median	Minimum	Maximum
Public	0.27	0.00	0.00	4.00
Private	0.63	0.00	0.00	3.00

Table 1.2D: Lectures or speeches

Public or Private	Mean	Median	Minimum	Maximum
Public	6.77	4.00	0.00	40.00
Private	3.50	1.50	0.00	12.00

Table 1.2E: Film or movie showings

Public or Private	Mean	Median	Minimum	Maximum
Public	2.09	0.00	0.00	20.00
Private	0.00	0.00	0.00	0.00

Table 1.2F: Fairs

Public or Private	Mean	Median	Minimum	Maximum
Public	0.82	0.00	0.00	6.00
Private	0.38	0.00	0.00	1.00

Table 1.2G: Exhibits

Public or Private	Mean	Median	Minimum	Maximum
Public	7.36	4.00	0.00	50.00
Private	3.25	1.50	0.00	14.00

Table 1.2H: Auctions

Public or Private	Mean	Median	Minimum	Maximum
Public	0.05	0.00	0.00	1.00
Private	0.00	0.00	0.00	0.00

Table 1.3: How many of each of the following kinds of special events did the library present in the past year? Broken out by type of college.

Table 1.3A: Readings

Type of College	Mean	Median	Minimum	Maximum
Community college	2.25	1.50	0.00	6.00
4-year college	2.40	3.00	0.00	5.00
MA-/PhD-granting college	2.57	1.00	0.00	10.00
Research university	2.44	0.00	0.00	10.00

Table 1.3B: Musical performances

Type of College	Mean	Median	Minimum	Maximum
Community college	0.00	0.00	0.00	0.00
4-year college	0.80	0.00	0.00	4.00
MA-/PhD-granting college	0.43	0.00	0.00	2.00
Research university	2.89	2.00	0.00	16.00

Table 1.3C: Theatrical performances

Type of College	Mean	Median	Minimum	Maximum
Community college	0.00	0.00	0.00	0.00
4-year college	0.60	0.00	0.00	4.00
MA-/PhD-granting college	0.14	0.00	0.00	1.00
Research university	0.44	0.00	0.00	3.00

Table 1.3D: Lectures or speeches

Type of College	Mean	Median	Minimum	Maximum
Community college	2.00	1.50	0.00	5.00
4-year college	2.80	1.50	0.00	10.00
MA-/PhD- granting college	4.43	4.00	0.00	10.00
Research university	12.22	12.00	0.00	40.00

Table 1.3E: Film or movie showings

Type of College	Mean	Median	Minimum	Maximum
Community college	0.50	0.00	0.00	2.00
4-year college	0.00	0.00	0.00	0.00
MA-/PhD- granting college	4.00	0.00	0.00	20.00
Research university	1.78	1.00	0.00	9.00

Table 1.3F: Fairs

Type of College	Mean	Median	Minimum	Maximum
Community college	0.75	0.50	0.00	2.00
4-year college	0.60	0.00	0.00	2.00
MA-/PhD- granting college	0.29	0.00	0.00	2.00
Research university	1.11	0.00	0.00	6.00

Table 1.3G: Exhibits

Type of College	Mean	Median	Minimum	Maximum
Community college	10.50	10.00	4.00	18.00
4-year college	6.80	1.50	0.00	50.00
MA-/PhD- granting college	4.14	3.00	1.00	12.00
Research university	5.44	5.00	0.00	14.00

Table 1.3H: Auctions

Type of College	Mean	Median	Minimum	Maximum
Community college	0.25	0.00	0.00	1.00
4-year college	0.00	0.00	0.00	0.00
MA-/PhD-granting college	0.00	0.00	0.00	0.00
Research university	0.00	0.00	0.00	0.00

Table 1.4: How many of each of the following kinds of special events did the library present in the past year? Broken out by average annual full-time student tuition.

Table 1.4A: Readings

Tuition	Mean	Median	Minimum	Maximum
Less than $10,000	1.36	1.00	0.00	6.00
$10,000 to $19,999	3.30	1.00	0.00	10.00
$20,000 or more	2.78	2.00	0.00	10.00

Table 1.4B: Musical performances

Tuition	Mean	Median	Minimum	Maximum
Less than $10,000	0.64	0.00	0.00	4.00
$10,000 to $19,999	2.40	0.00	0.00	16.00
$20,000 or more	0.67	0.00	0.00	2.00

Table 1.4C: Theatrical performances

Tuition	Mean	Median	Minimum	Maximum
Less than $10,000	0.36	0.00	0.00	4.00
$10,000 to $19,999	0.10	0.00	0.00	1.00
$20,000 or more	0.67	0.00	0.00	3.00

Table 1.4D: Lectures or speeches

Tuition	Mean	Median	Minimum	Maximum
Less than $10,000	4.73	2.00	0.00	19.00
$10,000 to $19,999	5.10	2.00	0.00	18.00
$20,000 or more	8.22	4.00	0.00	40.00

Table 1.4E: Film or movie showings

Tuition	Mean	Median	Minimum	Maximum
Less than $10,000	2.09	0.00	0.00	20.00
$10,000 to $19,999	2.00	0.00	0.00	9.00
$20,000 or more	0.33	0.00	0.00	3.00

Table 1.4F: Fairs

Tuition	Mean	Median	Minimum	Maximum
Less than $10,000	0.45	0.00	0.00	2.00
$10,000 to $19,999	0.90	0.00	0.00	6.00
$20,000 or more	0.78	1.00	0.00	2.00

Table 1.4G: Exhibits

Tuition	Mean	Median	Minimum	Maximum
Less than $10,000	9.82	4.00	0.00	50.00
$10,000 to $19,999	3.90	3.50	0.00	12.00
$20,000 or more	4.56	2.00	1.00	14.00

Table 1.4H: Auctions

Tuition	Mean	Median	Minimum	Maximum
Less than $10,000	0.09	0.00	0.00	1.00
$10,000 to $19,999	0.00	0.00	0.00	0.00
$20,000 or more	0.00	0.00	0.00	0.00

Table 1.5: How many of each of the following kinds of special events did the library present in the past year? Broken out by full-time equivalent enrollment.

Table 1.5A: Readings

Enrollment	Mean	Median	Minimum	Maximum
Less than 5,000	2.00	2.00	0.00	5.00
5,000 to 19,999	2.30	1.00	0.00	10.00
20,000 or more	3.11	1.00	0.00	10.00

Table 1.5B: Musical performances

Enrollment	Mean	Median	Minimum	Maximum
Less than 5,000	0.18	0.00	0.00	2.00
5,000 to 19,999	1.00	0.00	0.00	4.00
20,000 or more	2.78	1.00	0.00	16.00

Table 1.5C: Theatrical performances

Enrollment	Mean	Median	Minimum	Maximum
Less than 5,000	0.18	0.00	0.00	2.00
5,000 to 19,999	0.80	0.00	0.00	4.00
20,000 or more	0.11	0.00	0.00	1.00

Table 1.5D: Lectures or speeches

Enrollment	Mean	Median	Minimum	Maximum
Less than 5,000	1.91	1.00	0.00	10.00
5,000 to 19,999	4.80	4.50	0.00	12.00
20,000 or more	12.00	8.00	0.00	40.00

Table 1.5E: Film or movie showings

Enrollment	Mean	Median	Minimum	Maximum
Less than 5,000	0.18	0.00	0.00	2.00
5,000 to 19,999	0.80	0.00	0.00	8.00
20,000 or more	4.00	1.00	0.00	20.00

Table 1.5F: Fairs

Enrollment	Mean	Median	Minimum	Maximum
Less than 5,000	0.45	0.00	0.00	2.00
5,000 to 19,999	0.50	0.00	0.00	2.00
20,000 or more	1.22	0.00	0.00	6.00

Table 1.5G: Exhibits

Enrollment	Mean	Median	Minimum	Maximum
Less than 5,000	3.91	2.00	0.00	18.00
5,000 to 19,999	10.60	4.00	0.00	50.00
20,000 or more	4.33	4.00	0.00	9.00

Table 1.5H: Auctions

Enrollment	Mean	Median	Minimum	Maximum
Less than 5,000	0.00	0.00	0.00	0.00
5,000 to 19,999	0.10	0.00	0.00	1.00
20,000 or more	0.00	0.00	0.00	0.00

Table 1.6: How many of each of the following kinds of special events did the library present in the past year? Broken out by total number of special events presented by the library in the past year.

Table 1.6A: Readings

Number of Events	Mean	Median	Minimum	Maximum
Less than 10	1.27	1.00	0.00	5.00
10 or more	3.60	2.00	0.00	10.00

Table 1.6B: Musical performances

Number of Events	Mean	Median	Minimum	Maximum
Less than 10	0.00	0.00	0.00	0.00
10 or more	2.47	2.00	0.00	16.00

Table 1.6C: Theatrical performances

Number of Events	Mean	Median	Minimum	Maximum
Less than 10	0.00	0.00	0.00	0.00
10 or more	0.73	0.00	0.00	4.00

Table 1.6D: Lectures or speeches

Number of Events	Mean	Median	Minimum	Maximum
Less than 10	1.47	1.00	0.00	6.00
10 or more	10.33	8.00	0.00	40.00

Table 1.6E: Film or movie showings

Number of Events	Mean	Median	Minimum	Maximum
Less than 10	0.00	0.00	0.00	0.00
10 or more	3.07	1.00	0.00	20.00

Table 1.6F: Fairs

Number of Events	Mean	Median	Minimum	Maximum
Less than 10	0.20	0.00	0.00	2.00
10 or more	1.20	1.00	0.00	6.00

Table 1.6G: Exhibits

Number of Events	Mean	Median	Minimum	Maximum
Less than 10	2.53	2.00	0.00	6.00
10 or more	10.00	6.00	0.00	50.00

Table 1.6H: Auctions

Number of Events	Mean	Median	Minimum	Maximum
Less than 10	0.07	0.00	0.00	1.00
10 or more	0.00	0.00	0.00	0.00

If your library hosted any other kinds of special events in the past year, what were they and how many did they host?

10. Photo shoots 20, Movie Filming 5.

11. One Student Symposium, based on film, one guided exhibits tour.

12. Ten.

13. Six Orientation and Outreach Activities.

14. One.

15. Six.

16. Four.

17. Seven.

18. Free Coffee & Cookies during exam week; Books in the Baking (Edible Books Contest); Frisbee Golf in the Library.

19. One.

20. Four.

21. One.

22. Gala dinner (one).

23. Two: a reception to honor Dean and reunion of former student employees.

24. One.

25. Three.

26. Chess exhibition; woodturning exhibition.

Table 1.7: Does the library have a budget specifically for events?

	No Answer	Yes	No
Entire sample	0.00%	25.81%	74.19%

Table 1.8: Does the library have a budget specifically for events? Broken out by public or private status of the college.

Public or Private	Yes	No
Public	26.09%	73.91%
Private	25.00%	75.00%

Table 1.9: Does the library have a budget specifically for events? Broken out by type of college.

Type of College	Yes	No
Community college	25.00%	75.00%
4-year college	18.18%	81.82%
MA-/PhD-granting college	14.29%	85.71%
Research university	44.44%	55.56%

Table 1.10: Does the library have a budget specifically for events? Broken out by average annual full-time student tuition.

Tuition	Yes	No
Less than $10,000	25.00%	75.00%
$10,000 to $19,999	20.00%	80.00%
$20,000 or more	33.33%	66.67%

Table 1.11: Does the library have a budget specifically for events? Broken out by full-time equivalent enrollment.

Enrollment	Yes	No
Less than 5,000	27.27%	72.73%
5,000 to 19,999	18.18%	81.82%
20,000 or more	33.33%	66.67%

Table 1.12: Does the library have a budget specifically for events? Broken out by total number of special events presented by the library in the past year.

Number of Events	Yes	No
Less than 10	26.67%	73.33%
10 or more	25.00%	75.00%

Table 1.13: If so, what is this budget?

	Mean	Median	Minimum	Maximum
Entire sample	$7,200.00	$10,000.00	$600.00	$15,000.00

Table 1.14: If so, what is this budget? Broken out by public or private status of the college.

Public or Private	Mean	Median	Minimum	Maximum
Public	$7,920.00	$10,000.00	$600.00	$15,000.00
Private	$5,400.00	$5,400.00	$800.00	$10,000.00

Table 1.15: If so, what is this budget? Broken out by type of college.

Type of College	Mean	Median	Minimum	Maximum
Community college	$600.00	$600.00	$600.00	$600.00
4-year college	$1,400.00	$1,400.00	$800.00	$2,000.00
MA-/PhD-granting college	N/A	N/A	N/A	N/A
Research university	$11,750.00	$11,000.00	$10,000.00	$15,000.00

Table 1.16: If so, what is this budget? Broken out by average annual full-time student tuition.

Tuition	Mean	Median	Minimum	Maximum
Less than $10,000	$6,866.67	$10,000.00	$600.00	$10,000.00
$10,000 to $19,999	$15,000.00	$15,000.00	$15,000.00	$15,000.00
$20,000 or more	$4,933.33	$2,000.00	$800.00	$12,000.00

Table 1.17: If so, what is this budget? Broken out by full-time equivalent enrollment.

Enrollment	Mean	Median	Minimum	Maximum
Less than 5,000	$1,133.33	$800.00	$600.00	$2,000.00
5,000 to 19,999	$15,000.00	$15,000.00	$15,000.00	$15,000.00
20,000 or more	$10,666.67	$10,000.00	$10,000.00	$12,000.00

Table 1.18: If so, what is this budget? Broken out by total number of special events presented by the library in the past year.

Number of Events	Mean	Median	Minimum	Maximum
Less than 10	$6,950.00	$6,000.00	$800.00	$15,000.00
10 or more	$7,533.33	$10,000.00	$600.00	$12,000.00

Which departments of the library stage the most events and approximately how many do they stage each year?

1. Library Advancement Office is responsible for most events.

2. The College Library and the Young Research Library. I don't have the statistics for the Young Research Library. College Library stages about 15-20 per year.

3. Special Collections.

4. Director's office & Public Services in conjunction with academic departments and administrative units.

5. Outreach and Marketing (six).

6. We are usually hosting events 'staged' by other departments on campus. Occasionally we will 'stage' our own event, but are so small that it's not really assigned to a particular department.

7. Special Collections, 18.

8. This is a small library without departments.

9. External Relations - 90%.

10. Reference and instruction, 10-12.

11. User Experience coordinates the most events, but participation is library-wide. Exhibits are spread across a committee and individual departments.

12. Graduate Library - 20/year; Undergraduate Library - 12/year; Special Collections Library - 10/year. The Library also hosts and co-sponsors events with units throughout campus.

13. Marketing 16.

14. Reference @ 12.

15. Main Library-approx 30.

16. Entire library - we don't distinguish between departments. The marketing committee, however, is in charge of planning and organizing.

17. Library Communications - 2 major events per year.

18. Archives & Special Collections -- varies; this year was a particularly high number for us.

19. The library is not divided into departments.

20. Administration office and a variety of other library staff members as needed and as interested.

21. Development and Communication/most.

22. Research & Instructional Services (RIS) -- Learn at the Library lecture series -- 13 sessions Dean's Office -- Development & Outreach - 5 Engineering Library - 4 Learning Community Librarian/RIS – 1.

23. Circulation/Interlibrary Loan Services – 3.

24. Administration – 3.

Table 1.19: How many events did the library present in each of the following years?

Table 1.19A: 2011

	Mean	Median	Minimum	Maximum
Entire sample	14.97	8.00	1.00	80.00

Table 1.19B: 2012

	Mean	Median	Minimum	Maximum
Entire sample	18.50	12.00	2.00	73.00

Table 1.19C: 2013 (anticipated)

	Mean	Median	Minimum	Maximum
Entire sample	20.27	11.00	1.00	80.00

Table 1.20: How many events did the library present in each of the following years? Broken out by public or private status of the college.

Table 1.20A: 2011

Public or Private	Mean	Median	Minimum	Maximum
Public	17.74	10.00	1.00	80.00
Private	5.86	6.00	2.00	10.00

Table 1.20B: 2012

Public or Private	Mean	Median	Minimum	Maximum
Public	21.52	16.00	3.00	73.00
Private	8.57	7.00	2.00	22.00

Table 1.20C: 2013 (anticipated)

Public or Private	Mean	Median	Minimum	Maximum
Public	23.98	16.00	1.00	80.00
Private	9.14	8.00	1.00	25.00

Table 1.21: How many events did the library present in each of the following years? Broken out by type of college.

Table 1.21A: 2011

Type of College	Mean	Median	Minimum	Maximum
Community college	7.75	7.50	4.00	12.00
4-year college	11.91	6.00	2.00	50.00
MA-/PhD- granting college	11.71	5.00	1.00	35.00
Research university	25.63	20.00	2.00	80.00

Table 1.21B: 2012

Type of College	Mean	Median	Minimum	Maximum
Community college	11.50	9.50	7.00	20.00
4-year college	14.91	9.00	2.00	50.00
MA-/PhD- granting college	14.86	8.00	4.00	35.00
Research university	30.13	26.50	2.00	73.00

Table 1.21C: 2013 (anticipated)

Type of College	Mean	Median	Minimum	Maximum
Community college	13.13	8.75	5.00	30.00
4-year college	16.55	8.00	2.00	50.00
MA-/PhD- granting college	16.33	13.00	1.00	35.00
Research university	33.57	30.00	1.00	80.00

Table 1.22: How many events did the library present in each of the following years? Broken out by average annual full-time student tuition.

Table 1.22A: 2011

Tuition	Mean	Median	Minimum	Maximum
Less than $10,000	14.50	8.00	1.00	50.00
$10,000 to $19,999	15.20	11.00	2.00	40.00
$20,000 or more	15.38	7.00	2.00	80.00

Table 1.22B: 2012

Tuition	Mean	Median	Minimum	Maximum
Less than $10,000	17.75	12.00	2.00	50.00
$10,000 to $19,999	20.90	18.00	3.00	50.00
$20,000 or more	16.63	7.50	2.00	73.00

Table 1.22C: 2013 (anticipated)

Tuition	Mean	Median	Minimum	Maximum
Less than $10,000	18.96	10.00	1.00	50.00
$10,000 to $19,999	22.56	16.00	3.00	55.00
$20,000 or more	19.57	8.00	2.00	80.00

Table 1.23: How many events did the library present in each of the following years? Broken out by full-time equivalent enrollment.

Table 1.23A: 2011

Enrollment	Mean	Median	Minimum	Maximum
Less than 5,000	5.64	5.00	1.00	10.00
5,000 to 19,999	15.30	5.50	3.00	50.00
20,000 or more	26.00	20.00	2.00	80.00

Table 1.23B: 2012

Enrollment	Mean	Median	Minimum	Maximum
Less than 5,000	9.00	7.00	2.00	22.00
5,000 to 19,999	17.50	10.00	3.00	50.00
20,000 or more	31.22	27.00	2.00	73.00

Table 1.23C: 2013 (anticipated)

Enrollment	Mean	Median	Minimum	Maximum
Less than 5,000	10.27	8.00	1.00	30.00
5,000 to 19,999	19.39	8.00	3.00	50.00
20,000 or more	35.00	30.00	1.00	80.00

Table 1.24: How many events did the library present in each of the following years? Broken out by total number of special events presented by the library in the past year.

Table 1.24A: 2011

Number of Events	Mean	Median	Minimum	Maximum
Less than 10	4.33	5.00	1.00	8.00
10 or more	25.60	20.00	6.00	80.00

Table 1.24B: 2012

Number of Events	Mean	Median	Minimum	Maximum
Less than 10	6.07	6.00	2.00	12.00
10 or more	30.93	27.00	12.00	73.00

Table 1.24C: 2013 (anticipated)

Number of Events	Mean	Median	Minimum	Maximum
Less than 10	5.82	6.00	1.00	12.00
10 or more	34.71	30.00	6.00	80.00

Chapter 2: Revenue and Attendance

Table 2.1: For what percentage of events does the library charge admission?

	Mean	Median	Minimum	Maximum
Entire sample	0.63%	0.00%	0.00%	5.00%

Table 2.2: For what percentage of events does the library charge admission? Broken out by public or private status of the college.

Public or Private	Mean	Median	Minimum	Maximum
Public	0.85%	0.00%	0.00%	5.00%
Private	0.00%	0.00%	0.00%	0.00%

Table 2.3: For what percentage of events does the library charge admission? Broken out by type of college.

Type of College	Mean	Median	Minimum	Maximum
Community college	0.25%	0.00%	0.00%	1.00%
4-year college	0.00%	0.00%	0.00%	0.00%
MA-/PhD-granting college	1.21%	0.00%	0.00%	5.00%
Research university	1.11%	0.00%	0.00%	5.00%

Table 2.4: For what percentage of events does the library charge admission? Broken out by average annual full-time student tuition.

Tuition	Mean	Median	Minimum	Maximum
Less than $10,000	0.50%	0.00%	0.00%	5.00%
$10,000 to $19,999	1.35%	0.00%	0.00%	5.00%
$20,000 or more	0.00%	0.00%	0.00%	0.00%

Table 2.5: For what percentage of events does the library charge admission? Broken out by full-time equivalent enrollment.

Enrollment	Mean	Median	Minimum	Maximum
Less than 5,000	0.00%	0.00%	0.00%	0.00%
5,000 to 19,999	0.32%	0.00%	0.00%	2.50%
20,000 or more	1.78%	0.00%	0.00%	5.00%

Table 2.6: For what percentage of events does the library charge admission? Broken out by total number of special events presented by the library in the past year.

Number of Events	Mean	Median	Minimum	Maximum
Less than 10	0.07%	0.00%	0.00%	1.00%
10 or more	1.16%	0.00%	0.00%	5.00%

Table 2.7: What was the total attendance at all library-sponsored events in the past year?

	Mean	Median	Minimum	Maximum
Entire sample	1,198.40	600.00	80.00	5,000.00

Table 2.8: What was the total attendance at all library-sponsored events in the past year? Broken out by public or private status of the college.

Public or Private	Mean	Median	Minimum	Maximum
Public	1,500.56	1,000.00	80.00	5,000.00
Private	421.43	350.00	250.00	700.00

Table 2.9: What was the total attendance at all library-sponsored events in the past year? Broken out by type of college.

Type of College	Mean	Median	Minimum	Maximum
Community college	483.33	500.00	450.00	500.00
4-year college	601.00	325.00	80.00	3,000.00
MA-/PhD-granting college	1,783.33	1,000.00	100.00	5,000.00
Research university	1,966.67	1,600.00	600.00	4,000.00

Table 2.10: What was the total attendance at all library-sponsored events in the past year? Broken out by average annual full-time student tuition.

Tuition	Mean	Median	Minimum	Maximum
Less than $10,000	938.00	750.00	230.00	3,000.00
$10,000 to $19,999	1,766.25	1,500.00	80.00	5,000.00
$20,000 or more	921.43	350.00	300.00	4,000.00

Table 2.11: What was the total attendance at all library-sponsored events in the past year? Broken out by full-time equivalent enrollment.

Enrollment	Mean	Median	Minimum	Maximum
Less than 5,000	420.91	350.00	80.00	900.00
5,000 to 19,999	1,255.00	750.00	100.00	3,000.00
20,000 or more	2,225.00	1,600.00	600.00	5,000.00

Table 2.12: What was the total attendance at all library-sponsored events in the past year? Broken out by total number of special events presented by the library in the past year.

Number of Events	Mean	Median	Minimum	Maximum
Less than 10	460.83	400.00	80.00	1,000.00
10 or more	1,879.23	1,200.00	230.00	5,000.00

Table 2.13: What is the average attendance for each of the following types of events?

Table 2.13A: Readings

	Mean	Median	Minimum	Maximum
Entire sample	54.18	30.00	1.00	300.00

Table 2.13B: Musical performances

	Mean	Median	Minimum	Maximum
Entire sample	39.63	30.00	10.00	100.00

Table 2.13C: Theatrical performances

	Mean	Median	Minimum	Maximum
Entire sample	37.00	40.00	20.00	50.00

Table 2.13D: Lectures or speeches

	Mean	Median	Minimum	Maximum
Entire sample	56.62	40.00	10.00	300.00

Table 2.13E: Film or movie showings

	Mean	Median	Minimum	Maximum
Entire sample	36.00	21.50	5.00	150.00

Table 2.13F: Fairs

	Mean	Median	Minimum	Maximum
Entire sample	88.27	44.00	0.00	300.00

Table 2.13G: Exhibits

	Mean	Median	Minimum	Maximum
Entire sample	254.11	100.00	5.00	2,000.00

Table 2.13H: Auctions

	Mean	Median	Minimum	Maximum
Entire sample	75.00	75.00	75.00	75.00

Table 2.13I: All other

	Mean	Median	Minimum	Maximum
Entire sample	214.09	150.00	30.00	1,000.00

Table 2.14: What is the average attendance for each of the following types of events? Broken out by public or private status of the college.

Table 2.14A: Readings

Public or Private	Mean	Median	Minimum	Maximum
Public	61.92	40.00	1.00	300.00
Private	29.00	18.00	5.00	75.00

Table 2.14B: Musical performances

Public or Private	Mean	Median	Minimum	Maximum
Public	43.86	40.00	15.00	100.00
Private	10.00	10.00	10.00	10.00

Table 2.14C: Theatrical performances

Public or Private	Mean	Median	Minimum	Maximum
Public	46.67	50.00	40.00	50.00
Private	22.50	22.50	20.00	25.00

Table 2.14D: Lectures or speeches

Public or Private	Mean	Median	Minimum	Maximum
Public	45.24	40.00	10.00	100.00
Private	105.00	50.00	20.00	300.00

Table 2.14E: Film or movie showings

Public or Private	Mean	Median	Minimum	Maximum
Public	36.00	21.50	5.00	150.00
Private	N/A	N/A	N/A	N/A

Table 2.14F: Fairs

Public or Private	Mean	Median	Minimum	Maximum
Public	79.56	44.00	0.00	300.00
Private	127.50	127.50	5.00	250.00

Table 2.14G: Exhibits

Public or Private	Mean	Median	Minimum	Maximum
Public	298.86	100.00	20.00	2,000.00
Private	97.50	67.50	5.00	250.00

Table 2.14H: Auctions

Public or Private	Mean	Median	Minimum	Maximum
Public	75.00	75.00	75.00	75.00
Private	N/A	N/A	N/A	N/A

Table 2.14I: All other

Public or Private	Mean	Median	Minimum	Maximum
Public	222.50	125.00	30.00	1000.00
Private	191.67	175.00	50.00	350.00

Table 2.15: What is the average attendance for each of the following types of events? Broken out by type of college.

Table 2.15A: Readings

Type of College	Mean	Median	Minimum	Maximum
Community college	20.00	25.00	10.00	25.00
4-year college	41.88	42.50	1.00	80.00
MA-/PhD-granting college	135.33	100.00	6.00	300.00
Research university	40.00	40.00	30.00	50.00

Table 2.15B: Musical performances

Type of College	Mean	Median	Minimum	Maximum
Community college	N/A	N/A	N/A	N/A
4-year college	35.50	32.50	10.00	67.00
MA-/PhD-granting college	15.00	15.00	15.00	15.00
Research university	53.33	40.00	20.00	100.00

Table 2.15C: Theatrical performances

Type of College	Mean	Median	Minimum	Maximum
Community college	N/A	N/A	N/A	N/A
4-year college	30.00	30.00	20.00	40.00
MA-/PhD-granting college	N/A	N/A	N/A	N/A
Research university	41.67	50.00	25.00	50.00

Table 2.15D: Lectures or speeches

Type of College	Mean	Median	Minimum	Maximum
Community college	21.67	25.00	15.00	25.00
4-year college	39.86	40.00	10.00	69.00
MA-/PhD-granting college	52.00	50.00	30.00	100.00
Research university	97.50	62.50	20.00	300.00

Table 2.15E: Film or movie showings

Type of College	Mean	Median	Minimum	Maximum
Community college	15.00	15.00	15.00	15.00
4-year college	23.00	23.00	23.00	23.00
MA-/PhD-granting college	25.00	25.00	25.00	25.00
Research university	45.00	20.00	5.00	150.00

Table 2.15F: Fairs

Type of College	Mean	Median	Minimum	Maximum
Community college	40.00	40.00	0.00	80.00
4-year college	63.17	24.50	0.00	250.00
MA-/PhD-granting college	N/A	N/A	N/A	N/A
Research university	170.67	200.00	12.00	300.00

Table 2.15G: Exhibits

Type of College	Mean	Median	Minimum	Maximum
Community college	190.00	150.00	20.00	400.00
4-year college	101.86	83.00	5.00	250.00
MA-/PhD-granting college	223.20	100.00	26.00	750.00
Research university	725.00	100.00	75.00	2,000.00

Table 2.15H: Auctions

Type of College	Mean	Median	Minimum	Maximum
Community college	75.00	75.00	75.00	75.00
4-year college	N/A	N/A	N/A	N/A
MA-/PhD- granting college	N/A	N/A	N/A	N/A
Research university	N/A	N/A	N/A	N/A

Table 2.15I: All other

Type of College	Mean	Median	Minimum	Maximum
Community college	150.00	150.00	150.00	150.00
4-year college	85.00	50.00	30.00	175.00
MA-/PhD- granting college	100.00	100.00	100.00	100.00
Research university	308.33	175.00	50.00	1000.00

Table 2.16: What is the average attendance for each of the following types of events? Broken out by average annual full-time student tuition.

Table 2.16A: Readings

Tuition	Mean	Median	Minimum	Maximum
Less than $10,000	42.71	25.00	1.00	100.00
$10,000 to $19,999	91.20	40.00	6.00	300.00
$20,000 or more	33.20	25.00	5.00	75.00

Table 2.16B: Musical performances

Tuition	Mean	Median	Minimum	Maximum
Less than $10,000	36.75	32.50	15.00	67.00
$10,000 to $19,999	70.00	70.00	40.00	100.00
$20,000 or more	15.00	15.00	10.00	20.00

Table 2.16C: Theatrical performances

Tuition	Mean	Median	Minimum	Maximum
Less than $10,000	40.00	40.00	40.00	40.00
$10,000 to $19,999	50.00	50.00	50.00	50.00
$20,000 or more	31.67	25.00	20.00	50.00

Table 2.16D: Lectures or speeches

Tuition	Mean	Median	Minimum	Maximum
Less than $10,000	65.82	40.00	10.00	300.00
$10,000 to $19,999	58.75	57.50	20.00	100.00
$20,000 or more	38.33	40.00	20.00	50.00

Table 2.16E: Film or movie showings

Tuition	Mean	Median	Minimum	Maximum
Less than $10,000	20.75	21.50	15.00	25.00
$10,000 to $19,999	65.00	40.00	5.00	150.00
$20,000 or more	10.00	10.00	10.00	10.00

Table 2.16F: Fairs

Tuition	Mean	Median	Minimum	Maximum
Less than $10,000	49.75	59.50	0.00	80.00
$10,000 to $19,999	104.00	12.00	0.00	300.00
$20,000 or more	115.00	102.50	5.00	250.00

Table 2.16G: Exhibits

Tuition	Mean	Median	Minimum	Maximum
Less than $10,000	462.88	175.00	20.00	2000.00
$10,000 to $19,999	100.25	87.50	26.00	200.00
$20,000 or more	78.33	40.00	5.00	250.00

Table 2.16H: Auctions

Tuition	Mean	Median	Minimum	Maximum
Less than $10,000	75.00	75.00	75.00	75.00
$10,000 to $19,999	N/A	N/A	N/A	N/A
$20,000 or more	N/A	N/A	N/A	N/A

Table 2.16I: All other

Tuition	Mean	Median	Minimum	Maximum
Less than $10,000	125.00	125.00	100.00	150.00
$10,000 to $19,999	125.00	125.00	50.00	200.00
$20,000 or more	321.00	175.00	30.00	1000.00

Table 2.17: What is the average attendance for each of the following types of events? Broken out by full-time equivalent enrollment.

Table 2.17A: Readings

Enrollment	Mean	Median	Minimum	Maximum
Less than 5,000	34.33	18.00	5.00	80.00
5,000 to 19,999	42.14	25.00	1.00	100.00
20,000 or more	105.00	45.00	30.00	300.00

Table 2.17B: Musical performances

Enrollment	Mean	Median	Minimum	Maximum
Less than 5,000	10.00	10.00	10.00	10.00
5,000 to 19,999	44.00	50.00	15.00	67.00
20,000 or more	43.75	30.00	15.00	100.00

Table 2.17C: Theatrical performances

Enrollment	Mean	Median	Minimum	Maximum
Less than 5,000	20.00	20.00	20.00	20.00
5,000 to 19,999	32.50	32.50	25.00	40.00
20,000 or more	50.00	50.00	50.00	50.00

Table 2.17D: Lectures or speeches

Enrollment	Mean	Median	Minimum	Maximum
Less than 5,000	37.50	45.00	15.00	50.00
5,000 to 19,999	42.71	30.00	10.00	100.00
20,000 or more	83.13	55.00	20.00	300.00

Table 2.17E: Film or movie showings

Enrollment	Mean	Median	Minimum	Maximum
Less than 5,000	15.00	15.00	15.00	15.00
5,000 to 19,999	23.00	23.00	23.00	23.00
20,000 or more	41.67	22.50	5.00	150.00

Table 2.17F: Fairs

Enrollment	Mean	Median	Minimum	Maximum
Less than 5,000	68.00	5.00	0.00	250.00
5,000 to 19,999	39.67	44.00	0.00	75.00
20,000 or more	170.67	200.00	12.00	300.00

Table 2.17G: Exhibits

Enrollment	Mean	Median	Minimum	Maximum
Less than 5,000	200.00	80.00	5.00	750.00
5,000 to 19,999	99.83	91.50	26.00	200.00
20,000 or more	593.75	150.00	75.00	2,000.00

Table 2.17H: Auctions

Enrollment	Mean	Median	Minimum	Maximum
Less than 5,000	N/A	N/A	N/A	N/A
5,000 to 19,999	75.00	75.00	75.00	75.00
20,000 or more	N/A	N/A	N/A	N/A

Table 2.17I: All other

Enrollment	Mean	Median	Minimum	Maximum
Less than 5,000	101.00	100.00	30.00	175.00
5,000 to 19,999	250.00	250.00	150.00	350.00
20,000 or more	337.50	150.00	50.00	1,000.00

Table 2.18: What is the average attendance for each of the following types of events? Broken out by total number of special events presented by the library in the past year.

Table 2.18A: Readings

Number of Events	Mean	Median	Minimum	Maximum
Less than 10	46.00	25.00	6.00	100.00
10 or more	59.90	35.00	1.00	300.00

Table 2.18B: Musical performances

Number of Events	Mean	Median	Minimum	Maximum
Less than 10	N/A	N/A	N/A	N/A
10 or more	39.63	30.00	10.00	100.00

Table 2.18C: Theatrical performances

Number of Events	Mean	Median	Minimum	Maximum
Less than 10	N/A	N/A	N/A	N/A
10 or more	37.00	40.00	20.00	50.00

Table 2.18D: Lectures or speeches

Number of Events	Mean	Median	Minimum	Maximum
Less than 10	80.63	50.00	25.00	300.00
10 or more	41.85	40.00	10.00	100.00

Table 2.18E: Film or movie showings

Number of Events	Mean	Median	Minimum	Maximum
Less than 10	N/A	N/A	N/A	N/A
10 or more	36.00	21.50	5.00	150.00

Table 2.18F: Fairs

Number of Events	Mean	Median	Minimum	Maximum
Less than 10	85.00	5.00	0.00	250.00
10 or more	89.50	59.50	0.00	300.00

Table 2.18G: Exhibits

Number of Events	Mean	Median	Minimum	Maximum
Less than 10	193.44	100.00	15.00	750.00
10 or more	314.78	100.00	5.00	2,000.00

Table 2.18H: Auctions

Number of Events	Mean	Median	Minimum	Maximum
Less than 10	75.00	75.00	75.00	75.00
10 or more	N/A	N/A	N/A	N/A

Table 2.18I: All other

Number of Events	Mean	Median	Minimum	Maximum
Less than 10	101.00	100.00	30.00	175.00
10 or more	308.33	175.00	50.00	1,000.00

Table 2.19: What were the total revenues from the following sources through library events in the past year?

Table 2.19A: Admission fees for tickets

	Mean	Median	Minimum	Maximum
Entire sample	$16.67	$0.00	$0.00	$500.00

Table 2.19B: Donations specifically to attend fundraising events

	Mean	Median	Minimum	Maximum
Entire sample	$1,100.00	$0.00	$0.00	$20,000.00

Table 2.20: What were the total revenues from the following sources through library events in the past year? Broken out by public or private status of the college.

Table 2.20A: Admission fees for tickets

Public or Private	Mean	Median	Minimum	Maximum
Public	$22.73	$0.00	$0.00	$500.00
Private	$0.00	$0.00	$0.00	$0.00

Table 2.20B: Donations specifically to attend fundraising events

Public or Private	Mean	Median	Minimum	Maximum
Public	$1,500.00	$0.00	$0.00	$20,000.00
Private	$0.00	$0.00	$0.00	$0.00

Table 2.21: What were the total revenues from the following sources through library events in the past year? Broken out by type of college.

Table 2.21A: Admission fees for tickets

Type of College	Mean	Median	Minimum	Maximum
Community college	$125.00	$0.00	$0.00	$500.00
4-year college	$0.00	$0.00	$0.00	$0.00
MA-/PhD-granting college	$0.00	$0.00	$0.00	$0.00
Research university	$0.00	$0.00	$0.00	$0.00

Table 2.21B: Donations specifically to attend fundraising events

Type of College	Mean	Median	Minimum	Maximum
Community college	$750.00	$0.00	$0.00	$3,000.00
4-year college	$0.00	$0.00	$0.00	$0.00
MA-/PhD-granting college	$2,857.14	$0.00	$0.00	$20,000.00
Research university	$1,111.11	$0.00	$0.00	$10,000.00

Table 2.22: What were the total revenues from the following sources through library events in the past year? Broken out by average annual full-time student tuition.

Table 2.22A: Admission fees for tickets

Tuition	Mean	Median	Minimum	Maximum
Less than $10,000	$41.67	$0.00	$0.00	$500.00
$10,000 to $19,999	$0.00	$0.00	$0.00	$0.00
$20,000 or more	$0.00	$0.00	$0.00	$0.00

Table 2.22B: Donations specifically to attend fundraising events

Tuition	Mean	Median	Minimum	Maximum
Less than $10,000	$272.73	$0.00	$0.00	$3,000.00
$10,000 to $19,999	$3,000.00	$0.00	$0.00	$20,000.00
$20,000 or more	$0.00	$0.00	$0.00	$0.00

Table 2.23: What were the total revenues from the following sources through library events in the past year? Broken out by full-time equivalent enrollment.

Table 2.23A: Admission fees for tickets

Enrollment	Mean	Median	Minimum	Maximum
Less than 5,000	$0.00	$0.00	$0.00	$0.00
5,000 to 19,999	$45.45	$0.00	$0.00	$500.00
20,000 or more	$0.00	$0.00	$0.00	$0.00

Table 2.23B: Donations specifically to attend fundraising events

Enrollment	Mean	Median	Minimum	Maximum
Less than 5,000	$0.00	$0.00	$0.00	$0.00
5,000 to 19,999	$300.00	$0.00	$0.00	$3,000.00
20,000 or more	$3,333.33	$0.00	$0.00	$20,000.00

Table 2.24: What were the total revenues from the following sources through library events in the past year? Broken out by total number of special events presented by the library in the past year.

Table 2.24A: Admission fees for tickets

Number of Events	Mean	Median	Minimum	Maximum
Less than 10	$33.33	$0.00	$0.00	$500.00
10 or more	$0.00	$0.00	$0.00	$0.00

Table 2.24B: Donations specifically to attend fundraising events

Number of Events	Mean	Median	Minimum	Maximum
Less than 10	$200.00	$0.00	$0.00	$3,000.00
10 or more	$2,000.00	$0.00	$0.00	$20,000.00

Chapter 3: Most Effective Events

What are some of the library's most effective events in terms of raising the awareness level of library patrons or in raising money through donations or admission fees?

1. Our Friends of EKU Libraries Annual Dinner (in raising awareness for EKU Libraries).

2. Concerts and dances.

3. Artist's Book Symposium, Faculty Book Signing.

4. We don't charge.

5. Web pages.

6. Library hosted Lincoln, a traveling exhibit sponsored by ALA and the Constitution Center.

7. Posters.

8. We usually just do author readings in the library.

9. Awareness-raising lectures.

10. Book sales.

11. UNT Speaks Out Lecture Series; Edible Books Festival; International Gaming Day.

12. Library Book Sale; LIBS 101 recruitment displays.

13. Explore Your Library Day, New Student Orientation Tours were the most effective in terms of raising awareness. Fundraising is handled through other channels.

14. Any library event raises awareness--those we do in conjunction with other departments or academic divisions are effective.

15. Our Therapy Dog programs are by far our most popular in the Undergraduate Library. We reach hundreds of students each time we hold them. In the

Graduate Library, popular authors draw a large crowd, as well as programs that are specifically tied into one or more departments are popular.

16. Awareness: Readings / Lectures.

17. Web sites.

18. 6x/year Science Study Break, with faculty presenting research that is linked with current popular media Libraries Research Fair, all 11 libraries participate in April to showcase their collections and reference support for students.

19. Our Open House has been the most successful to date. Students also LOVE the annual Frisbee Golf Tournament.

20. Author lectures.

21. When the university as a whole becomes involved in organizing events around a theme, such as 2008 presidential debate on campus or 50th anniversary of integration or common book reading experience, related events in our department have higher attendance records due to class assignments. In addition, programs in the past related to legal and judicial collections have gathered large numbers because arrangements were made to give Continuing Legal Education credits for attendance.

22. We don't collect fees as a public institution; however, we have success with our newsletter and with direct appeals for donations of goods and services.

23. International Gaming Day is always popular and gets them to many parts of the library.

24. Art auction, Bingo, silent auction.

25. Gala Dinner with Friends.

26. We don't raise money with our events. They are for stewardship. We held an exhibit from a private collector last year and solicited attendees after the event for money to support special collections. It raised $5,170.

27. Hosted a traveling exhibit from the National Library of Medicine and organized an opening program.

28. Email, public television, fliers and mailers.

If your library shows films, what was the most popular film or film series presented by the library over the past three years?

1. We used to have an International Film Series, which was quite popular.

2. We showed the film Fordson: Faith, Fasting and Football recently with much success. In general, films are not very popular programming at the Library.

3. Feature films with particular (chosen) themes.

4. Girl Walk/All Day - screened on side of main library building during one of the first evenings of the school year; hip-hop dance followed.

5. "The Help," as a culminating event for a book club.

6. Science Fiction.

If your library holds book readings, what was the most popular reading that your library has staged over the past three years?

1. All book readings are somewhat successful; to name a few: Nancy Jensen, Silas House, and other local Kentucky authors have all been successful.

2. Only one: Lisa M. Stasse's "Unforgiven."

3. To Kill a Mockingbird.

4. Banned Books Week readings.

5. We have readings by our full-time and adjunct professors, or alumni, that are typically very popular.

6. We've only been co-sponsoring the Milton marathon (reading of Paradise Lost). It's very popular.

7. Creative Writing Department Faculty readings.

8. American Poetry.

9. Any reading by our faculty.

10. Economist Marina Whitman's reading from her autobiography this fall brought over 120 people to the Library.

11. Poetry.

12. N/A currently, we'd like to do these, possibly in partnership with Texas Book Festival. Working towards a modest series in 2012-2013.

13. Faculty reading their own works - these have been the most successful.

14. Poetry Day.

15. Local poets from local writer's guild.

16. A local author who is an outdoorsman.

17. Entertainers, such as Roy Blount Jr, Jud Hale.

Chapter 4: Staffing & Food Service

How does the library staff special events? Does the library incur additional fees for security, food service, usher services, or other personnel costs? What are the costs and how are they paid for?

1. Special events are staffed by library volunteers; most costs are paid through our special events account or foundation accounts as appropriate.

2. If there are security fees, they are paid for by the department. All other costs are absorbed by the library (it comes out of general funding).

3. Events staff help us. We have a budget for catering receptions. Average reception is $150.

4. No.

5. Library staff only.

6. Food Service & Extra Student Employees. Paid with endowment funds or grants.

7. Library staff, fees are covered by activity fund.

8. We set up, EKU has a catering service, cost for public is free.

9. We are small enough that we don't need any extra staffing.

10. For SC events, SC staff are expected to attend. Our budget covers catering, and publicity.

11. The readings are staffed by regular staff. There are no costs associated with the events.

12. There are no costs to the library. Most events are scheduled and then we work with the group scheduling the event.

13. Volunteers from library staff. Paid-staff time.

14. Library staff and student workers only; regular shifts.

15. We don't charge fees to provide staffing for events. In general, we provide tech

support for almost all events, and often have one additional staff member present to coordinate hosting the event. Our costs are primarily staff time (both tech and hosting) and in upkeep and maintenance for the facility and technology.

16. From general funds.

17. We staff with existing support staff and students when appropriate.

18. We use our own staff and student workers. We have not used our Food service or Catering on campus to date.

19. Typically 5-6 staff work events, plus student helpers. Additional costs for reception food and facilities.

20. Sometimes coffee and soft drinks provided for noon Brown Bag programs or evening programs. For special events, outside catering is hired. Paid for by library or department funds.

21. Rarely have food service, but when we do it is covered by our event budget.

22. No. Costs are minimal for some refreshments (less than $100 per event) unless we have a catered reception for an art exhibit which is $200-$300.

23. Volunteers from library for library events, and volunteers from the college for library fundraisers.

24. Varies.

25. Development & Outreach Librarian and one support staff member coordinates donor events, we engage catering, sometimes a student to staff the door. Catering is paid for out of the budget for the event, staffing is folded into the salaries of the Libraries.

26. Volunteer staff. Out of pocket for costs.

27. Facilities setup and breakdown - $400 for event Dining - $120.

Table 4.1: Does the library have an events coordinator or director who manages many of the executive functions of event preparation, marketing, and deployment?

	No Answer	Yes	No
Entire sample	6.45%	45.16%	48.39%

Table 4.2: Does the library have an events coordinator or director who manages many of the executive functions of event preparation, marketing, and deployment? Broken out by public or private status of the college.

Public or Private	No Answer	Yes	No
Public	8.70%	39.13%	52.17%
Private	0.00%	62.50%	37.50%

Table 4.3: Does the library have an events coordinator or director who manages many of the executive functions of event preparation, marketing, and deployment? Broken out by type of college.

Type of College	No Answer	Yes	No
Community college	25.00%	0.00%	75.00%
4-year college	0.00%	36.36%	63.64%
MA-/PhD-granting college	0.00%	42.86%	57.14%
Research university	11.11%	77.78%	11.11%

Table 4.4: Does the library have an events coordinator or director who manages many of the executive functions of event preparation, marketing, and deployment? Broken out by average annual full-time student tuition.

Tuition	No Answer	Yes	No
Less than $10,000	8.33%	33.33%	58.33%
$10,000 to $19,999	10.00%	60.00%	30.00%
$20,000 or more	0.00%	44.44%	55.56%

Table 4.5: Does the library have an events coordinator or director who manages many of the executive functions of event preparation, marketing, and deployment? Broken out by full-time equivalent enrollment.

Enrollment	No Answer	Yes	No
Less than 5,000	9.09%	27.27%	63.64%
5,000 to 19,999	0.00%	36.36%	63.64%
20,000 or more	11.11%	77.78%	11.11%

Table 4.6: Does the library have an events coordinator or director who manages many of the executive functions of event preparation, marketing, and deployment? Broken out by total number of special events presented by the library in the past year.

Number of Events	No Answer	Yes	No
Less than 10	6.67%	33.33%	60.00%
10 or more	6.25%	56.25%	37.50%

Table 4.7: How does the library generally handle food service at library special events?

	No answer	Does not offer food service	Provided by the college food service	Provided by the library café	Provided by outside caterers
Entire sample	3.23%	22.58%	51.61%	0.00%	22.58%

Table 4.8: How does the library generally handle food service at library special events? Broken out by public or private status of the college.

Public or Private	No answer	Does not offer food service	Provided by the college food service	Provided by the library café	Provided by outside caterers
Public	4.35%	13.04%	56.52%	0.00%	26.09%
Private	0.00%	50.00%	37.50%	0.00%	12.50%

Table 4.9: How does the library generally handle food service at library special events? Broken out by type of college.

Type of College	No answer	Does not offer food service	Provided by the college food service	Provided by the library café	Provided by outside caterers
Community college	25.00%	0.00%	50.00%	0.00%	25.00%
4-year college	0.00%	36.36%	54.55%	0.00%	9.09%
MA-/PhD-granting college	0.00%	14.29%	57.14%	0.00%	28.57%
Research university	0.00%	22.22%	44.44%	0.00%	33.33%

Table 4.10: How does the library generally handle food service at library special events? Broken out by average annual full-time student tuition.

Tuition	No answer	Does not offer food service	Provided by the college food service	Provided by the library café	Provided by outside caterers
Less than $10,000	8.33%	8.33%	66.67%	0.00%	16.67%
$10,000 to $19,999	0.00%	30.00%	50.00%	0.00%	20.00%
$20,000 or more	0.00%	33.33%	33.33%	0.00%	33.33%

Table 4.11: How does the library generally handle food service at library special events? Broken out by full-time equivalent enrollment.

Enrollment	No answer	Does not offer food service	Provided by the college food service	Provided by the library café	Provided by outside caterers
Less than 5,000	9.09%	45.45%	36.36%	0.00%	9.09%
5,000 to 19,999	0.00%	9.09%	72.73%	0.00%	18.18%
20,000 or more	0.00%	11.11%	44.44%	0.00%	44.44%

Table 4.12: How does the library generally handle food service at library special events? Broken out by total number of special events presented by the library in the past year.

Number of Events	No answer	Does not offer food service	Provided by the college food service	Provided by the library café	Provided by outside caterers
Less than 10	6.67%	26.67%	53.33%	0.00%	13.33%
10 or more	0.00%	18.75%	50.00%	0.00%	31.25%

Table 4.13: What was the library's spending for food service at all special events in the past year?

	Mean	Median	Minimum	Maximum
Entire sample	$1,991.67	$350.00	$0.00	$16,500.00

Table 4.14: What was the library's spending for food service at all special events in the past year? Broken out by public or private status of the college.

Public or Private	Mean	Median	Minimum	Maximum
Public	$2,441.67	$450.00	$0.00	$16,500.00
Private	$641.67	$150.00	$0.00	$3,000.00

Table 4.15: What was the library's spending for food service at all special events in the past year? Broken out by type of college.

Type of College	Mean	Median	Minimum	Maximum
Community college	$200.00	$200.00	$200.00	$200.00
4-year college	$192.86	$100.00	$0.00	$550.00
MA-/PhD-granting college	$1,166.67	$750.00	$0.00	$4,000.00
Research university	$4,338.89	$3,000.00	$0.00	$16,500.00

Table 4.16: What was the library's spending for food service at all special events in the past year? Broken out by average annual full-time student tuition.

Tuition	Mean	Median	Minimum	Maximum
Less than $10,000	$656.25	$225.00	$0.00	$3,000.00
$10,000 to $19,999	$3,730.00	$750.00	$0.00	$16,500.00
$20,000 or more	$875.00	$300.00	$0.00	$4,000.00

Table 4.17: What was the library's spending for food service at all special events in the past year? Broken out by full-time equivalent enrollment.

Enrollment	Mean	Median	Minimum	Maximum
Less than 5,000	$181.25	$150.00	$0.00	$550.00
5,000 to 19,999	$371.43	$300.00	$0.00	$1,000.00
20,000 or more	$4,861.11	$4,000.00	$0.00	$16,500.00

Table 4.18: What was the library's spending for food service at all special events in the past year? Broken out by total number of special events presented by the library in the past year.

Number of Events	Mean	Median	Minimum	Maximum
Less than 10	$535.00	$350.00	$0.00	$3,000.00
10 or more	$3,032.14	$625.00	$0.00	$16,500.00

Chapter 5: Departmental Help

Which academic or administrative departments of the college have partnered with the library to present special events at the library?

1. We partner with departments all over campus. Most of our readings take place through a partnership with the author's department (if an on-campus author).

2. School of Music, Undergraduate Research Center, student literary journal.

3. Printmaking, Fine Arts, Sequential Arts.

4. None.

5. President's Office, Advancement, Student Affairs, History, English, Visual Arts, Dance, Theater, Communication, Graphic Arts, Professional Development Center.

6. History department, English department.

7. Library advancement, the department that chairs the event.

8. English department.

9. English, History, Classics, German Studies, French Studies.

10. Creative Writing and Marketing.

11. School of Hospitality Management.

12. English department; History Department; Art Department.

13. Office of New Student and Family Programs, Kaplan Humanities Institute, Academic & Research Technologies, others departments as necessary.

14. Career Center, Admissions, Academic divisions (business, sciences, etc.), Campus Ministry, Student Success.

15. Many academic and administrative departments have partnered with the Library to offer events this year. Our partners range from individual academic departments on campus to centers and institutes, the president's office, central development for the University and occasionally community

organizations.

16. Alumni, Student Affairs.

17. History Department / Fine Arts Program.

18. Outreach and engagement.

19. College of Liberal Arts; Pharmacy; Psychology; Math; College of Fine Arts.

20. Career Services, Rhetoric Center, Campus Store (Book Store), English Department.

21. College of Sciences, College of Education, Mexico Center, Downtown Campus.

22. Gender Studies has utilized our space for weekly Brown Bag programs (but not considered Special Collections events as we are not involved in organizing and promoting). Do occasionally partner with conference organizers to host receptions in our space -- most often with Oxford Conference for the Book and the Faulkner Conference.

23. Academic Support Division, College Association, SGA.

24. Art department and Spiritual Formation.

25. Center for Teaching and Learning.

26. Humanities and Fine Arts; History.

27. University Foundation (fundraising arm of University), College of Arts & Sciences Office of Academic Affairs.

28. Student Health Services, Social Work Program.

29. New Hampshire Public Television.

Which departments of the college or other parent organization are essential as partners in managing a library-sponsored event?

1. The School of Music is an essential partner in our concert series.

2. Events staff.

3. Conservatory of Music.

4. Campus Catering, Alumni Affairs.

5. Depends on event.

6. The department that chairs an event Aramak-food shelving responsible for set up.

7. Creative Writing and Marketing.

8. Depends on the event.

9. Facilities.

10. Our partners vary based on the event, and we don't always bring partners in for events, though our events with partners tend to be the most successful.

11. Campus catering.

12. Special Events.

13. Newly created Events department of the Library, and if a particular event benefits a specific department of the university, generally that department will fully participate in the event planning and support.

14. We mostly do this on our own - I wouldn't say any dept. is "essential" to managing an event.

15. University Marketing, University Events.

16. Dean of Libraries; PR.

17. Academic Support Division, College Association, SGA.

18. For art exhibits, the art department.

19. Foundation.

20. Catering, building/facilities.

21. University Foundation (fundraising arm of University).

22. Administration Office.

Chapter 6: Marketing Library Special Events

Table 6.1: Do various library departments share lists of attendees of library special events for marketing purposes?

	No Answer	Yes	No
Entire sample	6.45%	22.58%	70.97%

Table 6.2: Do various library departments share lists of attendees of library special events for marketing purposes? Broken out by public or private status of the college.

Public or Private	No Answer	Yes	No
Public	8.70%	21.74%	69.57%
Private	0.00%	25.00%	75.00%

Table 6.3: Do various library departments share lists of attendees of library special events for marketing purposes? Broken out by type of college.

Type of College	No Answer	Yes	No
Community college	25.00%	0.00%	75.00%
4-year college	9.09%	9.09%	81.82%
MA-/PhD-granting college	0.00%	0.00%	100.00%
Research university	0.00%	66.67%	33.33%

Table 6.4: Do various library departments share lists of attendees of library special events for marketing purposes? Broken out by average annual full-time student tuition.

Tuition	No Answer	Yes	No
Less than $10,000	16.67%	16.67%	66.67%
$10,000 to $19,999	0.00%	30.00%	70.00%
$20,000 or more	0.00%	22.22%	77.78%

Table 6.5: Do various library departments share lists of attendees of library special events for marketing purposes? Broken out by full-time equivalent enrollment.

Enrollment	No Answer	Yes	No
Less than 5,000	9.09%	9.09%	81.82%
5,000 to 19,999	9.09%	0.00%	90.91%
20,000 or more	0.00%	66.67%	33.33%

Table 6.6: Do various library departments share lists of attendees of library special events for marketing purposes? Broken out by total number of special events presented by the library in the past year.

Number of Events	No Answer	Yes	No
Less than 10	6.67%	13.33%	80.00%
10 or more	6.25%	31.25%	62.50%

Are attendees at library special events generally encouraged or required to provide contact information such as addresses and email addresses so that the library can use them for event marketing purposes?

1. We typically ask for individuals to sign-in so that we can keep statistics of how many individuals attended. We might also send the individuals information about EKU Libraries, including our newsletter.

2. We now take reservations which require an email or phone number for contact information, but this isn't used for marketing. Attendees can opt to sign up for email notifications, but this is voluntary.

3. No.

4. Yes.

5. No.

6. No.

7. Not required.

8. Not to my knowledge.

9. No.

10. Yes. We encourage attendees to sign in. Development is also present at Special Collections events in order to encourage sign up for Friends of the Libraries.

11. No.

12. Mailing list sign ups are available. Card swiping for student attendance is currently being experimented with.

13. No, generally the events are designed for students and we already have student contact information.

14. No.

15. Yes--there's a sign-up sheet at each event.

16. Yes. We keep a mailing list for our main event space and typically have a sign up sheet posted at events.

17. Sometimes. Depends on the event.

18. No.

19. We request email address information at registration desk for all library events. While optional, it is strongly encouraged. Those emailed can opt-out of emailings (newsletters, etc.) at any time.

20. Only for our annual Open House. Attendees need to provide personal info in order to be eligible for prizes.

21. No.

22. For legal programs with CLE credit, sign-in sheets are required by the Bar Association and also utilized by department for future promotions of legal events.

23. No.

24. No. Our events are not for fundraising except for book sales.

25. We collect personal info for tax purposes at fund raisers and invite back past attendees to future fund raisers - for non fundraising events, we do not collect personal info.

26. Sometimes.

27. No.

28. Yes.

Table 6.7: How useful to your institution are the following marketing vehicles in advertising library special events?

Table 6.7A: Opt-in emails on all

	No Answer	Critical	Useful	Somewhat useful	Rarely useful	Unused/ Not useful
Entire sample	9.68%	12.90%	19.35%	9.68%	3.23%	45.16%

Table 6.7B: Ads in college newspapers

	No Answer	Critical	Useful	Somewhat useful	Rarely useful	Unused/ Not useful
Entire sample	9.68%	0.00%	25.81%	16.13%	6.45%	41.94%

Table 6.7C: Ads in commercial newspapers

	No Answer	Critical	Useful	Somewhat useful	Rarely useful	Unused/ Not useful
Entire sample	6.45%	6.45%	9.68%	9.68%	9.68%	58.06%

Table 6.7D: Postings on blogs and listservs

	No Answer	Critical	Useful	Somewhat useful	Rarely useful	Unused/ Not useful
Entire sample	3.23%	22.58%	25.81%	29.03%	3.23%	16.13%

Table 6.7E: Facebook or similar sites

	No Answer	Critical	Useful	Somewhat useful	Rarely useful	Unused/ Not useful
Entire sample	3.23%	22.58%	32.26%	25.81%	6.45%	9.68%

Table 6.7F: Twitter or similar sites

	No Answer	Critical	Useful	Somewhat useful	Rarely useful	Unused/ Not useful
Entire sample	16.13%	6.45%	19.35%	22.58%	6.45%	29.03%

Table 6.7G: YouTube or similar sites

	No Answer	Critical	Useful	Somewhat useful	Rarely useful	Unused/ Not useful
Entire sample	16.13%	0.00%	0.00%	29.03%	6.45%	48.39%

Table 6.7H: Pinterest or similar sites

	No Answer	Critical	Useful	Somewhat useful	Rarely useful	Unused/ Not useful
Entire sample	16.13%	0.00%	0.00%	16.13%	9.68%	58.06%

Table 6.7I: Library website

	No Answer	Critical	Useful	Somewhat useful	Rarely useful	Unused/ Not useful
Entire sample	6.45%	48.39%	35.48%	6.45%	0.00%	3.23%

Table 6.7J: Posters and flyers

	No Answer	Critical	Useful	Somewhat useful	Rarely useful	Unused/ Not useful
Entire sample	6.45%	54.84%	32.26%	6.45%	0.00%	0.00%

Table 6.7K: Presentations by librarians

	No Answer	Critical	Useful	Somewhat useful	Rarely useful	Unused/ Not useful
Entire sample	12.90%	9.68%	32.26%	19.35%	6.45%	19.35%

Table 6.7L: Emails to faculty and staff of the institution

	No Answer	Critical	Useful	Somewhat useful	Rarely useful	Unused/ Not useful
Entire sample	3.23%	51.61%	29.03%	9.68%	6.45%	0.00%

Table 6.8: How useful to your institution are the following marketing vehicles in advertising library special events? Broken out by public or private status of the college.

Table 6.8A: Opt-in emails

Public or Private	No Answer	Critical	Useful	Somewhat useful	Rarely useful	Unused/ Not useful
Public	13.04%	17.39%	13.04%	4.35%	4.35%	47.83%
Private	0.00%	0.00%	37.50%	25.00%	0.00%	37.50%

Table 6.8B: Ads in college newspapers

Public or Private	No Answer	Critical	Useful	Somewhat useful	Rarely useful	Unused/ Not useful
Public	13.04%	0.00%	21.74%	8.70%	8.70%	47.83%
Private	0.00%	0.00%	37.50%	37.50%	0.00%	25.00%

Table 6.8C: Ads in commercial newspapers

Public or Private	No Answer	Critical	Useful	Somewhat useful	Rarely useful	Unused/ Not useful
Public	4.35%	8.70%	8.70%	13.04%	8.70%	56.52%
Private	12.50%	0.00%	12.50%	0.00%	12.50%	62.50%

Table 6.8D: Postings on blogs and listservs

Public or Private	No Answer	Critical	Useful	Somewhat useful	Rarely useful	Unused/ Not useful
Public	4.35%	26.09%	26.09%	26.09%	4.35%	13.04%
Private	0.00%	12.50%	25.00%	37.50%	0.00%	25.00%

Table 6.8E: Facebook or similar sites

Public or Private	No Answer	Critical	Useful	Somewhat useful	Rarely useful	Unused/ Not useful
Public	4.35%	26.09%	26.09%	30.43%	8.70%	4.35%
Private	0.00%	12.50%	50.00%	12.50%	0.00%	25.00%

Table 6.8F: Twitter or similar sites

Public or Private	No Answer	Critical	Useful	Somewhat useful	Rarely useful	Unused/ Not useful
Public	17.39%	8.70%	17.39%	26.09%	8.70%	21.74%
Private	12.50%	0.00%	25.00%	12.50%	0.00%	50.00%

Table 6.8G: YouTube or similar sites

Public or Private	No Answer	Critical	Useful	Somewhat useful	Rarely useful	Unused/ Not useful
Public	17.39%	0.00%	0.00%	34.78%	8.70%	39.13%
Private	12.50%	0.00%	0.00%	12.50%	0.00%	75.00%

Table 6.8H: Pinterest or similar sites

Public or Private	No Answer	Critical	Useful	Somewhat useful	Rarely useful	Unused/ Not useful
Public	17.39%	0.00%	0.00%	21.74%	13.04%	47.83%
Private	12.50%	0.00%	0.00%	0.00%	0.00%	87.50%

Table 6.8I: Library website

Public or Private	No Answer	Critical	Useful	Somewhat useful	Rarely useful	Unused/ Not useful
Public	8.70%	52.17%	30.43%	4.35%	0.00%	4.35%
Private	0.00%	37.50%	50.00%	12.50%	0.00%	0.00%

Table 6.8J: Posters and flyers

Public or Private	No Answer	Critical	Useful	Somewhat useful	Rarely useful	Unused/ Not useful
Public	8.70%	52.17%	30.43%	8.70%	0.00%	0.00%
Private	0.00%	62.50%	37.50%	0.00%	0.00%	0.00%

Table 6.8K: Presentations by librarians

Public or Private	No Answer	Critical	Useful	Somewhat useful	Rarely useful	Unused/ Not useful
Public	8.70%	13.04%	39.13%	17.39%	4.35%	17.39%
Private	25.00%	0.00%	12.50%	25.00%	12.50%	25.00%

Table 6.8L: Emails to faculty and staff of the institution

Public or Private	No Answer	Critical	Useful	Somewhat useful	Rarely useful	Unused/ Not useful
Public	4.35%	65.22%	17.39%	8.70%	4.35%	0.00%
Private	0.00%	12.50%	62.50%	12.50%	12.50%	0.00%

Table 6.9: How useful to your institution are the following marketing vehicles in advertising library special events? Broken out by type of college.

Table 6.9A: Opt-in emails

Type of College	No Answer	Critical	Useful	Somewhat useful	Rarely useful	Unused/ Not useful
Community college	25.00%	25.00%	0.00%	0.00%	0.00%	50.00%
4-year college	9.09%	9.09%	18.18%	18.18%	0.00%	45.45%
MA-/PhD- granting college	0.00%	0.00%	14.29%	0.00%	14.29%	71.43%
Research university	11.11%	22.22%	33.33%	11.11%	0.00%	22.22%

Table 6.9B: Ads in college newspapers

Type of College	No Answer	Critical	Useful	Somewhat useful	Rarely useful	Unused/ Not useful
Community college	25.00%	0.00%	25.00%	25.00%	0.00%	25.00%
4-year college	9.09%	0.00%	36.36%	9.09%	0.00%	45.45%
MA-/PhD- granting college	0.00%	0.00%	14.29%	0.00%	28.57%	57.14%
Research university	11.11%	0.00%	22.22%	33.33%	0.00%	33.33%

Table 6.9C: Ads in commercial newspapers

Type of College	No Answer	Critical	Useful	Somewhat useful	Rarely useful	Unused/ Not useful
Community college	25.00%	0.00%	0.00%	25.00%	0.00%	50.00%
4-year college	9.09%	9.09%	9.09%	9.09%	9.09%	54.55%
MA-/PhD- granting college	0.00%	0.00%	0.00%	14.29%	14.29%	71.43%
Research university	0.00%	11.11%	22.22%	0.00%	11.11%	55.56%

Table 6.9D: Postings on blogs and listservs

Type of College	No Answer	Critical	Useful	Somewhat useful	Rarely useful	Unused/ Not useful
Community college	25.00%	0.00%	50.00%	0.00%	0.00%	25.00%
4-year college	0.00%	18.18%	27.27%	36.36%	0.00%	18.18%
MA-/PhD-granting college	0.00%	14.29%	28.57%	28.57%	14.29%	14.29%
Research university	0.00%	44.44%	11.11%	33.33%	0.00%	11.11%

Table 6.9E: Facebook or similar sites

Type of College	No Answer	Critical	Useful	Somewhat useful	Rarely useful	Unused/ Not useful
Community college	25.00%	0.00%	75.00%	0.00%	0.00%	0.00%
4-year college	0.00%	9.09%	54.55%	18.18%	0.00%	18.18%
MA-/PhD-granting college	0.00%	28.57%	14.29%	14.29%	28.57%	14.29%
Research university	0.00%	44.44%	0.00%	55.56%	0.00%	0.00%

Table 6.9F: Twitter or similar sites

Type of College	No Answer	Critical	Useful	Somewhat useful	Rarely useful	Unused/ Not useful
Community college	25.00%	0.00%	50.00%	0.00%	25.00%	0.00%
4-year college	27.27%	0.00%	9.09%	18.18%	0.00%	45.45%
MA-/PhD-granting college	0.00%	28.57%	0.00%	14.29%	14.29%	42.86%
Research university	11.11%	0.00%	33.33%	44.44%	0.00%	11.11%

Table 6.9G: YouTube or similar sites

Type of College	No Answer	Critical	Useful	Somewhat useful	Rarely useful	Unused/ Not useful
Community college	25.00%	0.00%	50.00%	50.00%	0.00%	25.00%
4-year college	27.27%	0.00%	9.09%	9.09%	0.00%	63.64%
MA-/PhD-granting college	0.00%	0.00%	0.00%	28.57%	14.29%	57.14%
Research university	11.11%	0.00%	33.33%	44.44%	11.11%	33.33%

Table 6.9H: Pinterest or similar sites

Type of College	No Answer	Critical	Useful	Somewhat useful	Rarely useful	Unused/ Not useful
Community college	25.00%	0.00%	0.00%	25.00%	25.00%	25.00%
4-year college	27.27%	0.00%	0.00%	18.18%	0.00%	54.55%
MA-/PhD-granting college	0.00%	0.00%	0.00%	0.00%	28.57%	71.43%
Research university	11.11%	0.00%	0.00%	22.22%	0.00%	66.67%

Table 6.9I: Library website

Type of College	No Answer	Critical	Useful	Somewhat useful	Rarely useful	Unused/ Not useful
Community college	25.00%	50.00%	25.00%	0.00%	0.00%	0.00%
4-year college	0.00%	54.55%	27.27%	9.09%	0.00%	9.09%
MA-/PhD-granting college	14.29%	42.86%	28.57%	14.29%	0.00%	0.00%
Research university	0.00%	44.44%	55.56%	0.00%	0.00%	0.00%

Table 6.9J: Posters and flyers

Type of College	No Answer	Critical	Useful	Somewhat useful	Rarely useful	Unused/ Not useful
Community college	25.00%	75.00%	0.00%	0.00%	0.00%	0.00%
4-year college	0.00%	63.64%	27.27%	9.09%	0.00%	0.00%
MA-/PhD-granting college	14.29%	42.86%	28.57%	14.29%	0.00%	0.00%
Research university	0.00%	44.44%	55.56%	0.00%	0.00%	0.00%

Table 6.9K: Presentations by librarians

Type of College	No Answer	Critical	Useful	Somewhat useful	Rarely useful	Unused/ Not useful
Community college	25.00%	25.00%	25.00%	25.00%	0.00%	0.00%
4-year college	27.27%	9.09%	9.09%	18.18%	9.09%	27.27%
MA-/PhD-granting college	0.00%	14.29%	71.43%	14.29%	0.00%	0.00%
Research university	0.00%	0.00%	33.33%	22.22%	11.11%	33.33%

Table 6.9L: Emails to faculty and staff of the institution

Type of College	No Answer	Critical	Useful	Somewhat useful	Rarely useful	Unused/ Not useful
Community college	25.00%	75.00%	0.00%	0.00%	0.00%	0.00%
4-year college	0.00%	36.36%	45.45%	18.18%	0.00%	0.00%
MA-/PhD-granting college	0.00%	57.14%	14.29%	14.29%	14.29%	0.00%
Research university	0.00%	55.56%	33.33%	0.00%	11.11%	0.00%

Table 6.10: How useful to your institution are the following marketing vehicles in advertising library special events? Broken out by average annual full-time student tuition.

Table 6.10A: Opt-in emails

Tuition	No Answer	Critical	Useful	Somewhat useful	Rarely useful	Unused/ Not useful
Less than $10,000	16.67%	25.00%	8.33%	0.00%	0.00%	50.00%
$10,000 to $19,999	10.00%	10.00%	20.00%	20.00%	10.00%	30.00%
$20,000 or more	0.00%	0.00%	33.33%	11.11%	0.00%	55.56%

Table 6.10B: Ads in college newspapers

Tuition	No Answer	Critical	Useful	Somewhat useful	Rarely useful	Unused/ Not useful
Less than $10,000	25.00%	0.00%	16.67%	16.67%	8.33%	33.33%
$10,000 to $19,999	0.00%	0.00%	40.00%	10.00%	10.00%	40.00%
$20,000 or more	0.00%	0.00%	22.22%	22.22%	0.00%	55.56%

Table 6.10C: Ads in commercial newspapers

Tuition	No Answer	Critical	Useful	Somewhat useful	Rarely useful	Unused/ Not useful
Less than $10,000	8.33%	8.33%	16.67%	8.33%	0.00%	58.33%
$10,000 to $19,999	0.00%	10.00%	10.00%	20.00%	20.00%	40.00%
$20,000 or more	11.11%	0.00%	0.00%	0.00%	11.11%	77.78%

Table 6.10D: Postings on blogs and listservs

Tuition	No Answer	Critical	Useful	Somewhat useful	Rarely useful	Unused/ Not useful
Less than $10,000	8.33%	33.33%	16.67%	25.00%	0.00%	16.67%
$10,000 to $19,999	0.00%	20.00%	30.00%	40.00%	10.00%	0.00%
$20,000 or more	0.00%	11.11%	33.33%	22.22%	0.00%	33.33%

Table 6.10E: Facebook or similar sites

Tuition	No Answer	Critical	Useful	Somewhat useful	Rarely useful	Unused/ Not useful
Less than $10,000	8.33%	25.00%	33.33%	25.00%	0.00%	8.33%
$10,000 to $19,999	0.00%	40.00%	10.00%	30.00%	10.00%	10.00%
$20,000 or more	0.00%	0.00%	55.56%	22.22%	11.11%	11.11%

Table 6.10F: Twitter or similar sites

Tuition	No Answer	Critical	Useful	Somewhat useful	Rarely useful	Unused/ Not useful
Less than $10,000	16.67%	8.33%	25.00%	16.67%	8.33%	25.00%
$10,000 to $19,999	10.00%	10.00%	20.00%	30.00%	0.00%	30.00%
$20,000 or more	22.22%	0.00%	11.11%	22.22%	11.11%	33.33%

Table 6.10G: YouTube or similar sites

Tuition	No Answer	Critical	Useful	Somewhat useful	Rarely useful	Unused/ Not useful
Less than $10,000	16.67%	0.00%	0.00%	25.00%	8.33%	50.00%
$10,000 to $19,999	10.00%	0.00%	0.00%	40.00%	10.00%	40.00%
$20,000 or more	22.22%	0.00%	0.00%	22.22%	0.00%	55.56%

Table 6.10H: Pinterest or similar sites

Tuition	No Answer	Critical	Useful	Somewhat useful	Rarely useful	Unused/ Not useful
Less than $10,000	16.67%	0.00%	0.00%	25.00%	16.67%	41.67%
$10,000 to $19,999	10.00%	0.00%	0.00%	20.00%	10.00%	60.00%
$20,000 or more	22.22%	0.00%	0.00%	0.00%	0.00%	77.78%

Table 6.10I: Library website

Tuition	No Answer	Critical	Useful	Somewhat useful	Rarely useful	Unused/ Not useful
Less than $10,000	8.33%	58.33%	25.00%	8.33%	0.00%	0.00%
$10,000 to $19,999	10.00%	40.00%	40.00%	0.00%	0.00%	10.00%
$20,000 or more	0.00%	44.44%	44.44%	11.11%	0.00%	0.00%

Table 6.10J: Posters and flyers

Tuition	No Answer	Critical	Useful	Somewhat useful	Rarely useful	Unused/ Not useful
Less than $10,000	8.33%	75.00%	8.33%	8.33%	0.00%	0.00%
$10,000 to $19,999	10.00%	30.00%	50.00%	10.00%	0.00%	0.00%
$20,000 or more	0.00%	55.56%	44.44%	0.00%	0.00%	0.00%

Table 6.10K: Presentations by librarians

Tuition	No Answer	Critical	Useful	Somewhat useful	Rarely useful	Unused/ Not useful
Less than $10,000	16.67%	25.00%	25.00%	25.00%	8.33%	0.00%
$10,000 to $19,999	10.00%	0.00%	50.00%	10.00%	0.00%	30.00%
$20,000 or more	11.11%	0.00%	22.22%	22.22%	11.11%	33.33%

Table 6.10L: Emails to faculty and staff of the institution

Tuition	No Answer	Critical	Useful	Somewhat useful	Rarely useful	Unused/ Not useful
Less than $10,000	8.33%	75.00%	8.33%	8.33%	0.00%	0.00%
$10,000 to $19,999	0.00%	40.00%	30.00%	20.00%	10.00%	0.00%
$20,000 or more	0.00%	33.33%	55.56%	0.00%	11.11%	0.00%

Table 6.11: How useful to your institution are the following marketing vehicles in advertising library special events? Broken out by full-time equivalent enrollment.

Table 6.11A: Opt-in emails

Enrollment	No Answer	Critical	Useful	Somewhat useful	Rarely useful	Unused/ Not useful
Less than 5,000	9.09%	0.00%	18.18%	18.18%	0.00%	54.55%
5,000 to 19,999	9.09%	27.27%	0.00%	0.00%	9.09%	54.55%
20,000 or more	11.11%	11.11%	44.44%	11.11%	0.00%	22.22%

Table 6.11B: Ads in college newspapers

Enrollment	No Answer	Critical	Useful	Somewhat useful	Rarely useful	Unused/ Not useful
Less than 5,000	9.09%	0.00%	36.36%	9.09%	0.00%	45.45%
5,000 to 19,999	9.09%	0.00%	27.27%	18.18%	18.18%	27.27%
20,000 or more	11.11%	0.00%	11.11%	22.22%	0.00%	55.56%

Table 6.11C: Ads in commercial newspapers

Enrollment	No Answer	Critical	Useful	Somewhat useful	Rarely useful	Unused/ Not useful
Less than 5,000	18.18%	0.00%	0.00%	9.09%	9.09%	63.64%
5,000 to 19,999	0.00%	18.18%	9.09%	18.18%	9.09%	45.45%
20,000 or more	0.00%	0.00%	22.22%	0.00%	11.11%	66.67%

Table 6.11D: Postings on blogs and listservs

Enrollment	No Answer	Critical	Useful	Somewhat useful	Rarely useful	Unused/ Not useful
Less than 5,000	9.09%	9.09%	27.27%	18.18%	0.00%	36.36%
5,000 to 19,999	0.00%	27.27%	36.36%	27.27%	9.09%	0.00%
20,000 or more	0.00%	33.33%	11.11%	44.44%	0.00%	11.11%

Table 6.11E: Facebook or similar sites

Enrollment	No Answer	Critical	Useful	Somewhat useful	Rarely useful	Unused/ Not useful
Less than 5,000	9.09%	0.00%	63.64%	0.00%	0.00%	27.27%
5,000 to 19,999	0.00%	36.36%	18.18%	27.27%	18.18%	0.00%
20,000 or more	0.00%	33.33%	11.11%	55.56%	0.00%	0.00%

Table 6.11F: Twitter or similar sites

Enrollment	No Answer	Critical	Useful	Somewhat useful	Rarely useful	Unused/ Not useful
Less than 5,000	27.27%	0.00%	9.09%	0.00%	9.09%	54.55%
5,000 to 19,999	18.18%	18.18%	18.18%	36.36%	9.09%	0.00%
20,000 or more	0.00%	0.00%	33.33%	33.33%	0.00%	33.33%

Table 6.11G: YouTube or similar sites

Enrollment	No Answer	Critical	Useful	Somewhat useful	Rarely useful	Unused/ Not useful
Less than 5,000	27.27%	0.00%	0.00%	9.09%	0.00%	63.64%
5,000 to 19,999	18.18%	0.00%	0.00%	45.45%	9.09%	27.27%
20,000 or more	0.00%	0.00%	0.00%	33.33%	11.11%	55.56%

Table 6.11H: Pinterest or similar sites

Enrollment	No Answer	Critical	Useful	Somewhat useful	Rarely useful	Unused/ Not useful
Less than 5,000	27.27%	0.00%	0.00%	0.00%	9.09%	63.64%
5,000 to 19,999	18.18%	0.00%	0.00%	27.27%	18.18%	36.36%
20,000 or more	0.00%	0.00%	0.00%	22.22%	0.00%	77.78%

Table 6.11I: Library website

Enrollment	No Answer	Critical	Useful	Somewhat useful	Rarely useful	Unused/ Not useful
Less than 5,000	9.09%	54.55%	18.18%	9.09%	0.00%	9.09%
5,000 to 19,999	9.09%	54.55%	36.36%	0.00%	0.00%	0.00%
20,000 or more	0.00%	33.33%	55.56%	11.11%	0.00%	0.00%

Table 6.11J: Posters and flyers

Enrollment	No Answer	Critical	Useful	Somewhat useful	Rarely useful	Unused/ Not useful
Less than 5,000	9.09%	63.64%	18.18%	9.09%	0.00%	0.00%
5,000 to 19,999	9.09%	54.55%	36.36%	0.00%	0.00%	0.00%
20,000 or more	0.00%	44.44%	44.44%	11.11%	0.00%	0.00%

Table 6.11K: Presentations by librarians

Enrollment	No Answer	Critical	Useful	Somewhat useful	Rarely useful	Unused/ Not useful
Less than 5,000	27.27%	0.00%	18.18%	27.27%	0.00%	27.27%
5,000 to 19,999	9.09%	27.27%	36.36%	0.00%	18.18%	9.09%
20,000 or more	0.00%	0.00%	44.44%	33.33%	0.00%	22.22%

Table 6.11L: Emails to faculty and staff of the institution

Enrollment	No Answer	Critical	Useful	Somewhat useful	Rarely useful	Unused/ Not useful
Less than 5,000	9.09%	36.36%	45.45%	9.09%	0.00%	0.00%
5,000 to 19,999	0.00%	63.64%	9.09%	9.09%	18.18%	0.00%
20,000 or more	0.00%	55.56%	33.33%	11.11%	0.00%	0.00%

Table 6.12: How useful to your institution are the following marketing vehicles in advertising library special events? Broken out by total number of special events presented by the library in the past year.

Table 6.12A: Opt-in emails

Number of Events	No Answer	Critical	Useful	Somewhat useful	Rarely useful	Unused/ Not useful
Less than 10	6.67%	6.67%	13.33%	13.33%	6.67%	53.33%
10 or more	12.50%	18.75%	25.00%	6.25%	0.00%	37.50%

Table 6.12B: Ads in college newspapers

Number of Events	No Answer	Critical	Useful	Somewhat useful	Rarely useful	Unused/ Not useful
Less than 10	6.67%	0.00%	20.00%	13.33%	13.33%	46.67%
10 or more	12.50%	0.00%	31.25%	18.75%	0.00%	37.50%

Table 6.12C: Ads in commercial newspapers

Number of Events	No Answer	Critical	Useful	Somewhat useful	Rarely useful	Unused/ Not useful
Less than 10	13.33%	6.67%	6.67%	6.67%	6.67%	60.00%
10 or more	0.00%	6.25%	12.50%	12.50%	12.50%	56.25%

Table 6.12D: Postings on blogs and listservs

Number of Events	No Answer	Critical	Useful	Somewhat useful	Rarely useful	Unused/ Not useful
Less than 10	6.67%	26.67%	33.33%	6.67%	6.67%	20.00%
10 or more	0.00%	18.75%	18.75%	50.00%	0.00%	12.50%

Table 6.12E: Facebook or similar sites

Number of Events	No Answer	Critical	Useful	Somewhat useful	Rarely useful	Unused/ Not useful
Less than 10	6.67%	20.00%	40.00%	0.00%	13.33%	20.00%
10 or more	0.00%	25.00%	25.00%	50.00%	0.00%	0.00%

Table 6.12F: Twitter or similar sites

Number of Events	No Answer	Critical	Useful	Somewhat useful	Rarely useful	Unused/ Not useful
Less than 10	26.67%	6.67%	13.33%	6.67%	6.67%	40.00%
10 or more	6.25%	6.25%	25.00%	37.50%	6.25%	18.75%

Table 6.12G: YouTube or similar sites

Number of Events	No Answer	Critical	Useful	Somewhat useful	Rarely useful	Unused/ Not useful
Less than 10	26.67%	0.00%	0.00%	6.67%	6.67%	60.00%
10 or more	6.25%	0.00%	0.00%	50.00%	6.25%	37.50%

Table 6.12H: Pinterest or similar sites

Number of Events	No Answer	Critical	Useful	Somewhat useful	Rarely useful	Unused/ Not useful
Less than 10	26.67%	0.00%	0.00%	0.00%	13.33%	60.00%
10 or more	6.25%	0.00%	0.00%	31.25%	6.25%	56.25%

Table 6.12I: Library website

Number of Events	No Answer	Critical	Useful	Somewhat useful	Rarely useful	Unused/ Not useful
Less than 10	13.33%	46.67%	26.67%	6.67%	0.00%	6.67%
10 or more	0.00%	50.00%	43.75%	6.25%	0.00%	0.00%

Table 6.12J: Posters and flyers

Number of Events	No Answer	Critical	Useful	Somewhat useful	Rarely useful	Unused/ Not useful
Less than 10	13.33%	53.33%	26.67%	6.67%	0.00%	0.00%
10 or more	0.00%	56.25%	37.50%	6.25%	0.00%	0.00%

Table 6.12K: Presentations by librarians

Number of Events	No Answer	Critical	Useful	Somewhat useful	Rarely useful	Unused/ Not useful
Less than 10	20.00%	6.67%	33.33%	13.33%	0.00%	26.67%
10 or more	6.25%	12.50%	31.25%	25.00%	12.50%	12.50%

Table 6.12L: Emails to faculty and staff of the institution

Number of Events	No Answer	Critical	Useful	Somewhat useful	Rarely useful	Unused/ Not useful
Less than 10	6.67%	46.67%	33.33%	6.67%	6.67%	0.00%
10 or more	0.00%	56.25%	25.00%	12.50%	6.25%	0.00%

What is your most effective way of marketing library special events?

1. Social media and word of mouth.

2. Emails to departments, library website, off-campus events websites.

3. Institution-wide email newsletter.

4. Email & Posters & direct mail.

5. Posters.

6. Email and posters.

7. Posters and flyers, Facebook.

8. Individual invitations.

9. Email to the academic community.

10. Faculty engagement almost guarantees attendance by students. Word of mouth is good for attendance but difficult to control.

11. Posting campus wide in the e-news bulletin.

12. Previous events, welcome tables, giant signs at the entrance.

13. Via library and college web pages.

14. Directly via email to a group of people with specific ties to or interest in an event.

15. It must be a combination of distribution methods.

16. Handsome posters.

17. Websites.

18. Press release to strategic media partners, save the date emails to donor list and those who have provided email at previous events; Facebook posts (depending on nature of the event and target demographic).

19. I cannot identify a MOST effective way. All taken together, (items checked above) we get the word out effectively!

20. Email, print ads.

21. Posting on university and community online calendars. For special events open to the public we will do press releases.

22. Enthusiasm via word of mouth.

23. Posters and announcements in Chapel.

24. Word of mouth and email.

25. Newsletter to 10,000 donors, faculty, and staff.

26. We mail invitations to the group of our donors. For instructional lectures done by librarians, we post on the Libraries website & social media sites. Some of the subject librarians may also promote their own lectures to the departments they liaison with.

27. University-wide memo.

28. New Hampshire Public Television.

Chapter 7: Library Events Staged Outside the Library

Table 7.1: How many special events sponsored at least in part by the library were held outside the library in the past year?

	Mean	Median	Minimum	Maximum
Entire sample	2.31	1.00	0.00	30.00

Table 7.2: How many special events sponsored at least in part by the library were held outside the library in the past year? Broken out by public or private status of the college.

Public or Private	Mean	Median	Minimum	Maximum
Public	2.95	1.00	0.00	30.00
Private	0.63	0.50	0.00	2.00

Table 7.3: How many special events sponsored at least in part by the library were held outside the library in the past year? Broken out by type of college.

Type of College	Mean	Median	Minimum	Maximum
Community college	1.00	0.00	0.00	3.00
4-year college	3.30	0.00	0.00	30.00
MA-/PhD-granting college	1.29	0.00	0.00	5.00
Research university	2.44	1.00	0.00	10.00

Table 7.4: How many special events sponsored at least in part by the library were held outside the library in the past year? Broken out by average annual full-time student tuition.

Tuition	Mean	Median	Minimum	Maximum
Less than $10,000	3.90	0.50	0.00	30.00
$10,000 to $19,999	2.30	1.00	0.00	10.00
$20,000 or more	0.56	0.00	0.00	2.00

Table 7.5: How many special events sponsored at least in part by the library were held outside the library in the past year? Broken out by full-time equivalent enrollment.

Enrollment	Mean	Median	Minimum	Maximum
Less than 5,000	0.60	0.00	0.00	3.00
5,000 to 19,999	3.90	0.00	0.00	30.00
20,000 or more	2.44	1.00	0.00	10.00

Table 7.6: How many special events sponsored at least in part by the library were held outside the library in the past year? Broken out by total number of special events presented by the library in the past year.

Number of Events	Mean	Median	Minimum	Maximum
Less than 10	0.57	0.00	0.00	3.00
10 or more	3.93	1.00	0.00	30.00

Please briefly describe these events.

1. Librarians sometimes take part in lecture series and other campus events and many times these are held outside library spaces. We also hold events for our donors which sometimes take place outside the library spaces.

2. Artist book symposium talks held in a larger auditorium on campus.

3. Plays, readings, exhibits, book discussions.

4. Lecture series.

5. One of our events is regularly held during a book festival. The venue is at the festival not in the library.

6. Art installation and partnership with the Kaplan Institute.

7. We hold events each year in recognition of Martin Luther King, Jr. Day which are too large for our event spaces in the Library. We typically hold these at other campus locations.

8. Community reads program.

9. Outside speaker/performer.

10. Off-site conferences sponsored by the Libraries, faculty talks; film screenings; libraries research fair.

11. We sponsored/organized a conference to be held on our campus and invited area librarians. Conference is entitled "Building a Bridge to College-Level Research." Area high schools join in. The idea is to share information and ideas re: college readiness of high school seniors.

12. Author lectures.

13. Clean Your Room Day began with a library display and evolved into a huge recycling effort. A civility sit-in was promoted via the library. Domestic Violence Awareness displays were part of a Dean of Students initiative.

14. Donor-related events in Boston, New York, DC.

15. A reception held in the University's Visitor's Center.

What was the approximate space rental cost, if any, for these events? If space was donated, mention this.

1. We have not encountered a space rental cost.

2. Space donated by home institution.

3. Donated space.

4. Space on campus did not incur cost.

5. The Festival sponsors this and I'm not aware of the cost.

6. Space hosted by campus partner.

7. $360.

8. $400-$500. Sometimes space is donated.

9. For conferences, space costs were approx $80/pp, per day. Costs recouped by registration fees. Other sites were on UT campus, no charge.

10. Approx. $250 for the event.

11. Minimal - used university facilities.

12. $0.

13. $3,000.

14. $400 for use of reception hall, plasma screen, tables and chairs.

Table 7.7: Approximately how many events that might be described as fundraisers did the library hold in the past year (including auctions, dinners, and any events designed to solicit donations or charity-related sales for the library)?

	Mean	Median	Minimum	Maximum
Entire sample	1.14	0.00	0.00	15.00

Table 7.8: Approximately how many events that might be described as fundraisers did the library hold in the past year (including auctions, dinners, and any events designed to solicit donations or charity-related sales for the library)? Broken out by public or private status of the college.

Public or Private	Mean	Median	Minimum	Maximum
Public	1.52	1.00	0.00	15.00
Private	0.00	0.00	0.00	0.00

Table 7.9: Approximately how many events that might be described as fundraisers did the library hold in the past year (including auctions, dinners, and any events designed to solicit donations or charity-related sales for the library)? Broken out by type of college.

Type of College	Mean	Median	Minimum	Maximum
Community college	0.33	0.00	0.00	1.00
4-year college	0.36	0.00	0.00	3.00
MA-/PhD-granting college	1.17	0.50	0.00	4.00
Research university	2.50	1.00	0.00	15.00

Table 7.10: Approximately how many events that might be described as fundraisers did the library hold in the past year (including auctions, dinners, and any events designed to solicit donations or charity-related sales for the library)? Broken out by average annual full-time student tuition.

Tuition	Mean	Median	Minimum	Maximum
Less than $10,000	0.64	0.00	0.00	3.00
$10,000 to $19,999	2.67	1.00	0.00	15.00
$20,000 or more	0.13	0.00	0.00	1.00

Table 7.11: Approximately how many events that might be described as fundraisers did the library hold in the past year (including auctions, dinners, and any events designed to solicit donations or charity-related sales for the library)? Broken out by full-time equivalent enrollment.

Enrollment	Mean	Median	Minimum	Maximum
Less than 5,000	0.10	0.00	0.00	1.00
5,000 to 19,999	0.89	0.00	0.00	4.00
20,000 or more	2.56	1.00	0.00	15.00

Table 7.12: Approximately how many events that might be described as fundraisers did the library hold in the past year (including auctions, dinners, and any events designed to solicit donations or charity-related sales for the library)? Broken out by total number of special events presented by the library in the past year.

Number of Events	Mean	Median	Minimum	Maximum
Less than 10	0.15	0.00	0.00	1.00
10 or more	2.00	1.00	0.00	15.00

Table 7.13: If the library did host any of these fundraising events, what percentage of the events were held in the library itself?

	Mean	Median	Minimum	Maximum
Entire sample	46.45%	50.00%	1.00%	100.00%

Table 7.14: If the library did host any of these fundraising events, what percentage of the events were held in the library itself? Broken out by public or private status of the college.

Public or Private	Mean	Median	Minimum	Maximum
Public	46.45%	50.00%	1.00%	100.00%
Private	N/A	N/A	N/A	N/A

Table 7.15: If the library did host any of these fundraising events, what percentage of the events were held in the library itself? Broken out by type of college.

Type of College	Mean	Median	Minimum	Maximum
Community college	1.00%	1.00%	1.00%	1.00%
4-year college	53.50%	53.50%	7.00%	100.00%
MA-/PhD-granting college	17.33%	1.00%	1.00%	50.00%
Research university	70.20%	100.00%	1.00%	100.00%

Table 7.16: If the library did host any of these fundraising events, what percentage of the events were held in the library itself? Broken out by average annual full-time student tuition.

Tuition	Mean	Median	Minimum	Maximum
Less than $10,000	14.75%	4.00%	1.00%	50.00%
$10,000 to $19,999	58.67%	75.00%	1.00%	100.00%
$20,000 or more	100.00%	100.00%	100.00%	100.00%

Table 7.17: If the library did host any of these fundraising events, what percentage of the events were held in the library itself? Broken out by full-time equivalent enrollment.

Enrollment	Mean	Median	Minimum	Maximum
Less than 5,000	100.00%	100.00%	100.00%	100.00%
5,000 to 19,999	19.33%	7.00%	1.00%	50.00%
20,000 or more	50.43%	50.00%	1.00%	100.00%

Table 7.18: If the library did host any of these fundraising events, what percentage of the events were held in the library itself? Broken out by total number of special events presented by the library in the past year.

Number of Events	Mean	Median	Minimum	Maximum
Less than 10	50.50%	50.50%	1.00%	100.00%
10 or more	45.56%	50.00%	1.00%	100.00%

Chapter 8: Records and Archives of Library Special Events

Are any library special events photographed or videotaped? If so, how do you use these photos or tapes and where are they presented or archived?

1. Always photographed -- then presented on Flickr, our webpage, through the University's electronic news system, and sometimes we also print and send copies to attendees as appropriate.

2. All of our concerts are photographed and many are videotaped. We use the photographs on our website and for other publicity, but the videos are usually recorded by the Music department or the performer. We usually get copies but they are not officially archived, although I would like that to happen. Some snippets are on YouTube.

3. Photographed, used on website, brochures, blog.

4. Facebook.

5. Photographed by university photographer.

6. Photographs, some are used in newsletters.

7. Videos are held in the library archives, photos are often seen on Facebook.

8. No.

9. Most are audio recorded and added to the website listing our events. (Special Collections)

10. No.

11. They are kept in the college archives here in the library.

12. Take pictures of special events and post on social media and website.

13. Yes. Library keeps photos to use in future marketing and to post on social media.

14. Yes. We regularly record events in our Graduate Library event space and store these videos on our website. We also occasionally have photographs taken for promotional or documentary purposes.

15. Yes. On the web, archived in database, and sometimes posted on YouTube.

16. Some.

17. Photographed by special events; used in promotional material.

18. Yes, all events are photographed. A few have been live streamed as well. We use YouTube to post videos, and use photos in newsletters, thank you cards, other library-related publications. They are maintained on our Libraries Flickr page.

19. Yes - photographed. We let people know this and ask for permission to take photos. The photos are presented on the library's Facebook site, and they also appear on the library's website and blog.

20. Yes - uploaded to YouTube and link shared with partners. Copy to University Archives.

21. Cataloged for archives; used in promotional publications and on website.

22. Used in our newsletter and posted online via Facebook.

23. No.

24. Yes, we photograph fund raising events and post selected photos to blog, FB, and website.

25. As much as possible, YouTube and archived at the library.

26. Photos are taken, used in donor newsletter. Archived in the office on CD.

27. Photographed. Not archived.

28. Yes, use them throughout the year to promote in display cases or on web.

If photos, video or audio tapes, or text transcripts of library special events are archived or otherwise maintained, has the library developed metadata or other finding aids so that these archives can be easily used? If so, how have you done this?

1. No, folder level description only.

2. No.

3. To a limited extent.

4. Videos are cataloged.

5. Some tapes are in the circulation area; they use to be in Periodicals.

6. No.

7. There is a finding aid.

8. No.

9. No metadata.

10. We use basic metadata to identify our videos. They are searchable via the Library's website.

11. Yes. But I don't know how.

12. Content DM.

13. I have not personally done so; our communications officer maintains the Flickr and YouTube pages, he uses tags as finding aids.

14. No, we have not.

15. MARC records.

16. Not yet.

17. Only on internal network directories - not in college archive.

Made in the USA
Lexington, KY
30 January 2013